15 GOOD REASONS
NOT TO GO TO CHURCH
AND ONE GREAT REASON
YOU SHOULD

15 GOOD REASONS
Not to Go to Church

And One Great Reason
YOU SHOULD

MICHAEL J. INSALACO

VMI Publishers • Sisters, Oregon

Published by
VMI Publishers
Sisters, Oregon
www.vmipublishers.com

ISBN: 9781935265078
ISBN: 1935265075

Library of Congress: 2009929477

Printed in the USA

Cover design by Joe Bailen

CONTENTS

PART THREE
CHECKING OUT CHRISTIAN CHURCHES ONE STEP AT A TIME

ACKNOWLEDGEMENTS

THERE ARE SOME WONDERFUL PEOPLE I have to acknowledge as vital contributors to this book. Without them, it might not have been published or even completed. Because of them, it is a better book than I could have ever managed on my own.

To my wife, Mitchie, who not only put up with my long hours of writing but was my greatest supporter in this effort: I love you. Thank you for your understanding and belief that this was something I needed to write. And thank you for keeping me in your constant prayer. You are the one woman on this earth I want to make proud. I hope I have.

To Sue Miholer, my editor at VMI: Thank you for being "picky, picky." Your mastery of the English language and your knowledge of the Christian faith have made this book better on both fronts.

To Bill Carmichael and Lacey Hanes Ogle of VMI Publishers: Thank you for believing in my manuscript. I hope, because of your belief, this book helps many people on the most important journey of their lives. (Thanks also for assigning Sue Miholer to edit it!)

To Rod Willis: Thanks for constructive criticism of the manuscript. Rod, thanks especially for asking me this critical question when I was unsure of whether to continue the investment of time and money: "If one person, whom you may never meet, reads this book and finds it helpful in his journey toward Christ, would it all be worth it to you?" The answer was "Yes." Thanks to you, Rod, the uncertainty ended there.

To Pastor Scott Borman: Thank you for helping me identify the "15 Good Reasons" and for your belief that this is a message that needs to be read by tentative explorers and the committed Christians and pastors who seek to reach out to them. Your passion and support was much-needed fuel for my tank.

To Jason Strickland: Thanks for finding ways to help and for being a trusted sounding board for my ideas.

To the men in my Bible study and prayer group and to my other close friends who have prayed and encouraged me as I wrote this book: Thanks for always having my back and helping to keep me focused on what is important.

And my ultimate thanks go to Jesus Christ for saving me, a sinner.

Dedication

For Mitchie, my wife,
best friend and sister in Christ.
You are a light to everyone you meet.
Especially to Mia and me.

PREFACE

I'M A CHRISTIAN. That means I'm a follower of Christ. I also go to church. And I'd love for you to follow Christ and go to church. I lay that out on the table so you don't read on under false pretenses. That having been said, and as the title of this book implies, I acknowledge that there are a lot of good reasons not to go to church. I know this because I was not always a Christian, nor did I always go to church.

I used to not go to church for all the same good reasons, perhaps, that you don't. I believed in my interpretation of God and had a generally favorable impression of Jesus most of my life. But I was no follower, and attending church regularly was something other people did.

Then there came a point in my life when I knew something was missing. Maybe that's where you are now. Quite honestly, I knew in my heart that the world's values and explanations for what makes life worth living weren't cutting it. And I had some inclination that this Jesus was someone I should know more about. I figured it was worth getting past all my reasons not to go to church because church was where they talked about this Jesus. So I hesitantly went to church. I went to church, expecting to roll my eyes, poke holes in sermons and make fun of people who bought into the whole Christianity thing completely. But I went.

For a while, I rolled my eyes, poked holes in sermons and made fun of people who bought into the whole Christianity thing completely. Then, after a while, I realized I enjoyed church. The things I was learning actually made more intelligent sense than the things the world had been teaching me. I was becoming a better man. I wanted to do the right thing even when no one was watching. I liked myself a lot more. And later, after a while more, I realized that I had just been enjoying the icing. The cake was something better than all that other good stuff put together. I found Jesus. I didn't just know of Him anymore. I knew Him. I asked Him to let me follow Him. And I haven't let go of Him since.

That was in 1991. I'm still going to church, still unfolding the mystery, still on a challenging journey with other people trying to do the same thing. It's from this perspective that I recently looked back at how it all began and decided to write this book for people who are just like I was. If you're thinking about going to church, skeptical of church, and not sure how deep you want to go into this whole Jesus thing, great! You're sane. You're honest. But at least you're open and thinking about it. So I'm writing to you the way I wish someone had written to me about church when I was kicking the idea around. When I say, "I can relate, man," I really can.

I'm going to give you straightforward information to think about, to think differently about, and to look into as you consider the possibility of going to church. I offer a very tangible step-by-step process of sticking your toes in the water. I think wading in little by little, if that's your style, is a perfectly respectable way of trying church. Cannonballs into uncertain waters are not for everyone.

By way of housekeeping, let me just handle a bit of terminology now so we don't get hung up on it throughout the book. Since this book is about church, and specifically a Christian church, let's define what church means. Church can be an individual church, like the one you mean when you ask, "Isn't that a lovely church?" In that instance, church is the building on the corner. If you say, "I like that church," you could also be referring to the reputation it has in the community or what you observe when you attend. Or you could say in more general terms, "I think I'll go to church this Sunday," meaning you're planning to go to a place where people meet to worship and study the Bible.

Another meaning for church is the entire body of Christian believers around the world—past, present and future. This one is also often referred to as "His church." The "His," of course, is referring to Jesus. It's His church. He paid for it through His death, burial and resurrection. It should be pretty evident from the context which "church" I'm referencing when I bounce back and forth with the term.

Here's a style issue I'd like to get out of the way. When I write about an undisclosed individual other than "you" or "me," I'm going to use the universal "him" to represent a "him" or a "her." It's far less cumbersome than writing "him or her" three times in the same sentence. And it's far more pleasant than using "undisclosed individual of either gender." I'm not a chauvinist. I just like pleasant sentences. Please don't be offended if your "him" is a "her." Just make your mental substitution, and realize you'd probably do the same thing if you were writing a book.

Now to more salient disclosures. I write this book with the premise that the reader—you—is at least toying with the idea of going to a Christian church, one that is part of His church. In chapter 1, I lay out a few litmus test items that true Christian churches have in common.

Since I am a Christian and believe that the Jesus Christ of the Christian Bible is God, I won't apologize for only recommending that you visit Christian churches. I know what Christ has done for me and how the Christian church has helped me learn about Him and become more like Him. I've still got plenty of rough edges, so it's a work-in-progress. But I know I'm not good enough or bright enough to have gotten this far on my own. And that's just here and now.

I also believe I'll spend eternity in heaven, rather than hell, because He loved me, died to pay the price for my sins, and rose again to live and reign forever. That's a lot for one sentence. Don't worry if you're not so sure about all that right now. But I believe it with all my heart. It's life-changing, life-defining stuff. And I'm assuming your interest in church might have something to do with wanting to find life-changing, life-defining stuff. So, bottom line, why would I send you anywhere else but to where I found it?

If you were in the market for a perfect nose job, and I had had a perfect nose job, I wouldn't send you to a podiatrist. I'd send you to my perfect-nose doc. I can't let you go out there thinking I've said, "All roads lead to God," or "Just get to church—any church—and you'll be better off." It's not true, and I wouldn't say it.

With that, let's jump into a bunch of good reasons not to go to church.

PART ONE

15 Good Reasons Not to Go to Church

I Don't Know What Makes a Church a "Christian" Church

When examining the list of good reasons some people don't go to church, one seems to rise to the top. New explorers of the Christian faith often don't know what makes a church a "Christian" church. Furthermore, there are so many denominations within the Christian church that even the most willing explorer might struggle with determining which is the right one for him. Baptist, Southern Baptist, General Baptist, Episcopalian, Lutheran, Catholic (Roman, Greek or Armenian), Pentecostal, Methodist, and, just to throw you off, non-denominational. And these are just *some* of the denominations! This denomination jungle doesn't make it easy for regular folks like you and me to try a church. It's intimidating. I'm intimidated, undereducated and confused about all the denominations, and I'm longtime Christian and churchgoer.

Well, let me eliminate all the confusion for you with one clear and concise answer about which denomination you should try: *There is no clear, concise answer.*

What? You're thinking about returning this book to get your money back? Okay, let me see if I can give you something more helpful as you look for a Christian church to try.

I won't tell you which denomination to choose. It's my contention that Christ allowed different denominations to flourish for His own purposes. He's a big God, so He's not afraid of variety. I believe there are assets and shortcomings in almost every denomination and different styles appeal to different people. I believe there are truly saved and committed followers of Christ in every Christian denomination. I believe Christ does not hold the shortcomings of a Christian denomination against truly saved and committed believers within the denomination who are just doing their best to follow Him.

While we should always do our best to learn and to separate His truth from wrong teaching, He knows we don't all start with perfect understanding. As we mature in our knowledge and reliance on the Holy Spirit, we become better equipped to decide if a particular pastor, a particular church or a particular denomination aligns with our understanding of His truth.

When questions arise, that's the time to find out if we are in error or if the teaching is in error. My goal is not to endorse one Christian denomination over another. It's to help you get started in exploring the Christian faith. You should be aware that there are some differences in teaching from one denomination to another. But don't feel like you have to understand every possible nuance before you start your journey.

That being said, I do want to help you start exploring in a church that solidly teaches the core beliefs that clearly make a Christian church a Christian church. If you find a church that does not agree with the beliefs I mention below, it's not a Christian church even if it bills itself as such. Look for these things, regardless of the denominations of the churches you are exploring:

- Jesus Christ is the head of the church
- There is one God made up of three persons: Jesus Christ (the Son), the Father and the Holy Spirit. It's an impossible concept to grasp fully. And I'm not going to even try to explain it in this book. I'm still trying to get my arms around it myself. It's perfectly okay to show up at church with a lot of questions about this. But do make sure any church you attend believes it and teaches it.
- The only way to be forgiven of your sins and go to a holy heaven after your earthly death is through faith in Christ and acceptance of His death on the cross as payment for your sins. You cannot do

enough good things to get yourself into heaven. You have to accept it as a gift. This is known as receiving salvation or becoming saved. Don't avoid going to church because you haven't made this step of faith. It's okay to go to church just to look into it, like I did. But, again, make sure any church you attend teaches this. If anyone tells you salvation comes from faith in Christ as your Savior "plus" anything else—being baptized, earning it through good works, being a member of one specific church or denomination, giving the church all your possessions or wearing magical love beads—he's wrong. One note on this, lest I leave you thinking I'm down on baptism. Far from it. Baptism is a wonderful expression to God and others that God, in His Word, asks of those who have professed Him as Savior and Lord. But baptism is not a requirement of salvation. On the day He died on the cross, Jesus granted forgiveness and salvation to a repentant thief dying on the cross next to him. All the thief did was admit that he was a sinner and profess his faith in Jesus as Savior and Lord. Jesus promised him, "Today, you will be with me in Paradise." Jesus didn't lie. That sinner was saved without ever having had the opportunity to be baptized. I was baptized as an adult to express publicly my gratitude for Christ's gift of salvation, not to gain it.

• Jesus died on the cross to pay for our sins. But He didn't stay dead. He rose again three days later. He is alive today preparing a place for His followers in heaven. He will return in all His glory one day. And His followers will experience a similar resurrection. This is great news for His followers. This is very bad news for anyone who says "no thanks" to what He offers freely.

• There is a literal heaven and a literal hell. All we really know about either is what the Bible reveals. I wouldn't rely on depictions on television, movies or comic books. My guess is that Satan, a fallen angel who wants God's glory for himself, is far too cunning and vain to wear a cheap rented red suit and carry a pitchfork. But he is real, and he would love to keep you from discovering how much God really loves you. He'd love for you to share his eternal misery outside of heaven. Heaven is only for those who have accepted Christ as Lord and Savior, because He is the only one capable of offering it and the only one who loved us enough to suffer for our sins on the cross. Heaven is a love-filled eternity with God. Hell is an eternity without God. The despair of this will likely be worse than any other tormenting that might happen there. To review, heaven and hell are real. Heaven is indescribably good. Hell is indescribably bad. (For the record, I've chosen heaven and would absolutely love to chat with you there some day.)

- The Bible is the accurate Word of God, written by men who were inspired by the Holy Spirit. It should be the focus of teaching in any Christian church. The Bible consists of the 66 books of the Old Testament (39) and the New Testament (27). While there are many translations of this one Bible, no other revelations or writings are necessary or helpful to add to God's revelation in the Bible. In fact, there are stern warnings by God that anyone who tries to add to or subtract from God's revelation will be judged harshly. Don't fall into the trap of reading any other "alternative Gospels" or attending a church that believes in them.

This list is not exhaustive or complete. But for your purposes, these are the big few that should point you in a good direction toward finding a true Christian church. My intention in this book is to help you get started, not to overwhelm you with doctrine. Plus, I'm not a leading authority on doctrine. I'm still learning to discern truth from untruth, myself. Remember, it's a process, not a brain transplant.

In chapter 18, I encourage you to do some simple research to compare the various Christian denominations and help you decide which might be a good fit for you.

CHAPTER TWO

I Know Too Many Church-Going Hypocrites

Hypocrites are everywhere. It's true. If a hypocrite is a person who says one thing and does another, the church is loaded with them. Pastors, church staff members, and the guys who direct traffic in the parking lots are all a bunch of hypocrites. And don't get me started on the people in the pews. I know a guy at my church who says "amen" when the pastor talks about forgiving others as you'd want to be forgiven. Then that same guy gets bent out of shape pulling out of the church parking lot because someone cuts him off. And that guy is writing a book to people about how great church can be!

Yeah, well, I'm not proud of it. But I'm a hypocrite. And since I'm being honest, can you be honest? Don't you have a little hypocrite DNA in you, too? Sure you do. Humans are hypocrites. We say we believe one thing and then act as if we believe something else. My best friends are hypocrites. If they weren't, they'd be inhuman. Part of the human condition is that we all struggle with selfishness, pride and a bunch of other negative attitudes that don't just go away once we cross the threshold of a church or accept Jesus into our lives. Point blank, if there were no hypocrites in church, there'd be no church.

To say you would not go to church because you know too many church-going hypocrites is simply not being fair to yourself or to church. I admit there are hypocrites that really tick me off. I have a real problem with people who are big and loud about their massive holiness—and your lack thereof—then cheat on a business deal or have an affair. That's just not normal, everyday, run-of-the-mill hypocrisy. It's the kind of hypocrisy that makes thinking people say, "If that's what God and the church is about, I don't want it."

But that's not what God or the church is about, so we should not attribute it to God and the church. Our hypocrisy goes against God's desire for us and against what you'll learn in a good church. Should those really irritating hypocrites keep you from enjoying what God and church can offer you? No way. That guy I mentioned earlier—the one who cheated on a business deal (maybe you know him)—may go to church, but he's not representing God with his behavior. He might be saved by God's grace. He might not be. We're all works-in-progress, even after we're saved. But don't deny yourself a better life just because he's not setting a good example.

Let God handle the judging and the consequences of hypocrisy. He forgives me. He'll forgive you. He'll even forgive the hypocrites who tick me off—if they really want or understand they need His forgiveness. If you've decided church might be a good thing for you or your family, be glad that God and churches accept hypocrites. There's always room for more.

Rest assured that hypocrites of all levels and shortcomings will be at church every Sunday. I'll be the one giving you a phony smile if you cut me off in the parking lot. What can I say? I'm a hypocrite.

They Just Want Money

Our income is very dear to us. It ought to be. Money is hard to earn and hard to save. Life is expensive. So when we hear of churches asking for money, we often have defensive reactions. The barriers to giving increase even more when we hear of church leaders paying for lavish lifestyles with their parishioners' donations. Even when they say the Bible teaches that Christians should be the wealthiest people on earth because Christians inherit all of God's blessings, something rings hollow. Let me offer a recommendation: Don't give a dime to any church or church leader that uses your money on excessive living. By "excessive," I mean ornate mansions, yachts, helicopters and gold-plated jump suits.

God does promise to meet a believer's needs and indeed He chooses in His wisdom to bless some believers with worldly wealth. But He does not promise that every believer will have excessive material wealth while they are here on earth. Some of us will have to wait to live like kings until we are with the King in heaven. I mistrust church leaders who teach otherwise. The worthy goals of contributing to a church are to support its ministry, to cover operating expenses, to pay its staff well so they can focus on God's work rather than holding three jobs, and to expand the kingdom of God. When the leaders of a church are overly focused on excessive personal wealth—and using too much of the church's income to support it—their priorities are askew. They themselves are not focused on the right reasons for giving money to the church. But when we hear of church leaders who abuse finances this way, it is important to remember that they represent a very small percentage of church leaders throughout the world.

There are also wealthy Christian leaders who have done nothing wrong. They may earn more money than Bill Gates—okay, that's a stretch—but they haven't done it by skimming donations from regular folks like you and me. Their wealth comes from other sources, such as book and video sales, wise investments or family inheritances. There's nothing wrong with anyone being wealthy if they do it the right way. Yet, we are predisposed to think badly of any church leaders who drive nice cars even though they receive modest salaries from their churches and give a huge portion of their own wealth back to the work of God. They shouldn't be maligned. They should be applauded as examples of using God's money God's way.

Despite what you may read or hear, don't assume that all churches are greedy for their own gain. It is simply not the overwhelming reality. Most churches are members of independent financial auditing organizations to help allay this perception. Most churches open their books to their church members. Most churches are trying to do great things for their parishioners, neighborhoods, communities and the world while being careful with every penny. Most church leaders, pastors and staffs are sadly underpaid for the work they do. And many parishioners don't give as much as they can or should in return. That's the overwhelming reality.

I don't know a pastor of a good Christian church that likes to preach about money or urge their parishioners to give. They'd much rather focus on the work of God than to address the church's need for money to pay for the work.

The real issue is how church attendees view money. Do they see it as a gift from God that they willingly reinvest in His work? Do church attendees want to help their church bless others as they've been blessed? Do they want the church's air conditioning and lights to be working at next Sunday's service? It all takes money. God provides us 100% of the money we have to pay for our own needs and to give us the opportunity use a portion of it to support His work. He doesn't need our investment. He wants it. He knows that how we spend our money is one of the greatest indicators of what we really care about. He'd like us to care about Him and His church. But He wants us to come to that conclusion.

It's more about allowing us the privilege and joy of willful participation in His work than it is about taking anything away from us. Discovering this perspective for ourselves is a greater purpose for giving to our churches than any of the others I mentioned.

If we could all view giving this way, pastors wouldn't have to remind us or ask for a penny. But we don't all view giving this way. Some of us are simply early in our learning processes on the issue. Others of us understand the concept well, but years of practice have cramped our hands around our wallets, our minds around our own desires, and our hearts around other things we love more than God's work.

If you find yourself bristling when a church asks its congregation to give, try to think differently about it than you may have in the past. Do we bristle when other organizations that champion the causes we love ask for money? Whether it's wiping out illiteracy, saving the whales, finding a cure for AIDS, or donating to a family that just lost everything in a fire, if we care about it, we don't get mad at those organizations for asking for our financial help. Yet, because of bad press and a small percentage of bad apples, churches are often not given the same consideration.

Actually, I think that most of us struggle with the concept of giving due to pure, old-fashioned selfishness. It's just that the relatively few well-publicized church abuses provide us a convenient justification for holding back. Most churches' programs have a tremendously positive impact on people's lives. And a church's income directly impacts its ability to bring the life-saving good news of God's forgiveness to people who thirst for it. This is a cause that affects people's eternities. If we can begin to think about giving to a church in these terms, we will, in time, respond differently to the request.

Make no mistake that when we refocus our minds to His desires, our hearts and hands will follow. God makes it clear that giving should come from the heart—responding to the privilege and joy I mentioned earlier.

You might not show up at church for the first time believing this principle and ready to participate in this way. That's perfectly okay. When the collection basket passes by, let it pass by. You should never give out of guilt or to impress the guy collecting the baskets. There won't be any thugs in the back waiting to roll you for cash on your way out. Nor will a self-righteous church lady sitting behind you whack you with her clutch purse. If one does, whack her back.

Over time, however, I hope you want to give to your church—and for all the right reasons. God hopes so too. It'll show you that your mind, heart and hands are changing. And it's a great feeling.

CHAPTER FOUR

Too Many Pastors
Have Abused Their Positions

When a pastor commits a crime, has an affair, engages in sexual misconduct, or otherwise abuses his position, the world loves to hear the details in the press and shout, "See! I told you they're all corrupt!"

Indeed, these are serious offenses worthy of punishment by the church and the authorities when appropriate. But they are the offenses of one person against another person, against God and against His church. They are not indicative of God and His church. In much the same way people use a pastor's misuse of money as a reason not to give money to any church, people who already don't want to attend church are quick to point to these wayward pastors as a reason they should not attend any church. Again, I point out that while there are far too many of these cases—each getting its fair share of play in the press—they do not represent the great majority of pastors or Christian churches.

If you're thinking of attending a Christian church but find yourself hesitating because of stories of fallen pastors, let me encourage you to consider a different perspective on this issue. Don't let the misdeeds of a few color your perception of the majority. The real fact of the matter is that most pastors work very hard to earn the trust of their flocks. They are normal, flawed people—just like you and me. Yet they know they are held to a higher standard because of their positions as representatives of Christ and teachers of His Word. They ask for, and receive, a higher level of accountability even in their private lives because they know they are as capable of falling as you and me. And they know that if they fall, they won't damage just their own lives, they'll damage the perception of Christ's church.

If you're genuine about your openness to attending church, you will have no problem finding one with a dedicated pastor. They make up the majority of pastors, not the minority. Even churches whose pastors have been guilty of serious offenses should not be held accountable for the pastor's actions, unless they retain the pastor in his role of leadership. In a right-thinking Christian church, a pastor who is indeed guilty of punishable misdeeds will be removed from pastoral activities immediately. If the pastor repents, seeks forgiveness and willfully offers any restitution required, he may remain in the loving arms of his congregation as he rehabilitates. Perhaps at some future time, he may be given pastoral duties again. These are all courtesies you and I should expect from our church families if we fall. If the pastor does not willfully repent, he'll be asked to leave the church. The new pastor will understand that his own faithfulness will be under greater scrutiny because of the actions of his predecessor. A Christian church might not be immune from pastoral abuses, but it is decidedly proactive in dealing with them.

Here's another thing to think about the next time you hear of a fallen pastor. Pastors are not, and should not become, the object of anyone's faith. That honor belongs only to God since He is the only one worthy of it. Any good pastor will tell you that. In fact, if you attend a church where the pastor seems to be seeking worship or personal glory rather than continually redirecting any praises to Jesus, I'd say you've got a potential fallen pastor on your hands. I've been going to church for a lot of years. I've visited perhaps 50 churches in that time and have called three of them home. In all those opportunities to run across a bad egg, I cannot recall once being in the presence of a pastor I thought was seeking worship for himself. I've only visited one church whose pastor later ended up in a scandal, and he was immediately removed from leadership when it came to light.

So, you see, very few Christian churches have a problem with fallen pastors. And the few that do usually deal with them decisively and require increased accountability in the future. The chances of you landing at a church in the midst of such strife are extremely low. Even if this issue should arise at the church you attend, it still doesn't change the fact that God is good and the Christian church is His instrument of good. It just means that a very visible person in the church made bad choices that were outside of God's will and the Bible's instruction. It should not, for one moment, lead you to the thought that God is not good and that His church is not His instrument of good.

I have great respect and appreciation for the senior pastor and the associate pastors at my church. They genuinely love God and give everything they have to teach His Word. I often share my appreciation with them in person or in e-mails. They deserve it. But while I admire them greatly, I will never worship them. Only God gets my worship, because only He deserves it.

Unlike God, pastors are human, made of flesh and blood. They struggle with the same character flaws, temptations and desires with which I struggle. They have the added burden of being under far more scrutiny from far more people than I am. Too many people expect them to be perfect, which is a heavy load to carry.

Pastors are under even heavier attack from Satan because they are actively equipping their parishioners to stand against him. I don't offer these observations to say we should look the other way if a pastor is found to be guilty of a serious offense. But I do urge you to have the same compassion you would want if you committed a serious offense. The consequences of a pastor's immoral behavior will be sure and swift. The embarrassment for the pastor, the people around him and his church will be heavy. But if we are worshipping God rather than a pastor, our worship of God will continue even when a pastor errs.

If one of my pastors should ever be guilty of a serious crime or abuse of his position, I would be hurt. But I hope I would be one of the first to put my arm around him and say, "You messed up. You need to get right with God and those you've hurt. But you're human. I could have just as easily done what you did. I love you. You've helped me get right with God through the years. What can I do to help you, brother?" His actions would never cause me to lose faith in God or to distrust all Christian churches.

If you have ever pointed to fallen pastors as a reason not to go to any Christian church, I hope you now have a clearer perspective. It's a relatively rare problem. And you shouldn't go to church to worship a person, anyway. Save that for God.

CHAPTER FIVE

I Don't Know the Drill;
They Do

ooking and feeling like "the new guy" can be a crippling prospect. You start your first day of a new job and look around. Everyone else has been there at least a couple of years. They buzz around you like a well-oiled machine while you wonder if you even sat in the right cubicle. You're afraid to sharpen your pencil because you might do it wrong and somehow disrupt the precision timing of their finely-tuned gears. And, of course, when it happens, you know they'll all screech to a halt, drop their files and stare at you with disapproving glares. A bead of sweat will roll down your forehead as you slowly slide down your chair to hide under your desk.

That's the kind of expectation a lot of people have about attending a church for the first time. They think that everyone else at church has been there forever and has had time to hone the critically important and monumentally sacred "church attendee routine." Of course, a major part of this routine is to stare disapprovingly at the new guys when they mess it up. This fear can be so great in some people that it is the single reason they don't go to church. If this sounds like you, I have fantastic news for you: No one cares.

Well, that didn't sound right. When people get to know you, they will care for you. But when you show up for the first time, you won't be the center of attention. Maybe someone will shake your hand and say, "Are you new here? Great to have you." Then when the service starts everyone will be focused on the service—not you. Even the church lady sitting directly behind you will be leaning to see around you to the stage or altar. No one there is depending on you to know or do anything. If the church does have some memorized responses, other attendees probably won't even notice if you don't chime in. The worst-case scenario is that the church lady sitting behind you actually is grading your performance and whacks you with her purse again. Whack her back again. If someone else's church experience becomes about evaluating yours, they've got bigger problems than you do.

There are some Christian denominations, like the Catholic church, that have more scripted responses from parishioners. When the priest says "X," the church responds "Y." Even in that situation, until you learn the responses, don't feel like you have to fake them. The future of the church isn't depending on you.

The real truth of the matter is that most Christian churches have absolutely no parishioner routine you can't easily pick up by listening to the pastor and sneaking a peek to your right. It'll be perfectly clear when it's time to stand up, sit down, shake hands, pass the collection plate and leave for a nice brunch somewhere.

Another fear that holds some people back from church is that they'll be singled out to talk or answer a question. I've never seen that happen in larger churches. At most, a pastor might ask the visitors to stand up or raise their hands so the church can welcome them with a round of applause.

In a smaller church, the pastor might address you directly. But it'll likely be as benign as, "I see some new faces here today. You, there, would you mind introducing yourself to us?"

Your response can be as simple as, "My name's Susan. I'm new to church and just visiting." (Please don't use "Susan" if your name is "Jake." That would just be unfriendly and a tad awkward.) But don't feel like you have to say more than that or say something "spiritual." Now, if a pastor does, for some inexplicable and completely unheard-of reason, ask you to come to the front of the church and recite the first five chapters of Deuteronomy from memory, just say what I'd say: "That's why you get the big bucks, Pastor. Go for it." Don't worry. It won't happen—I hope.

I would like to prepare you in advance for one thing that does seem to have caught on in a lot of churches. It's an epidemic that won't go away soon enough for my liking. In fact, I'd like a few minutes alone with the pastor that got this one started. Here it is. A pastor will make a statement—something like, "We all need a lot of forgiveness." It's a great point, and you'll just be absorbing it when he ruins the moment by saying, "Turn to your neighbor and say, 'You need a lot of forgiveness.'"

I've been going to church a long time, and this one still catches me off guard. I'm pretty sure I just have an attitude problem, but I don't like turning to my neighbor and saying anything somebody told me to tell him. If you don't have a problem with it, go for it. I think I'm the only one at my church that dislikes it. Everyone seems to have a good laugh and loosens up when it happens. Not me. I tighten up like a drum.

Thankfully, my wife is usually sitting right beside me. She knows when this happens, she is required to turn toward me quickly so I can ignore the guy on the other side of me. If she turns the other way, I give her the cold shoulder the rest of the day. It's in the contract.

But, there are times when we're not together, so I've developed an avoidance technique I'd like to pass along if you think this drill might make you equally uncomfortable. Always make sure you have something in your hands or on your lap during the service: a notepad, a pair of glasses, a Tiffany lamp—whatever. As soon as you hear the pastor utter the magic words, "Turn to your neighbor and say—," drop your prop on the floor with as much noise and commotion as possible and then lurch quickly to pick it up. Make sure you fumble with it on the floor long enough so there's no chance your "neighbor" will still be waiting for you when you come back up for air. Works like a charm.

If you get caught off guard without a prop, try faking a mild heart attack. A coughing fit or a good sneeze with a nose-blowing finish usually works, too. Desperate avoidance calls for desperate measures. Maybe, just maybe, if enough of us are dropping priceless lamps and having disruptive medical conditions every time a pastor does this, we will stop this epidemic once and for all. If you think I'm just being uptight about the whole thing, you're probably right. You can just ignore this warning and join in the fun. But if you're like me, you'll be thanking me for this tip someday.

Seriously, if any of these "new guy" fears are holding you back from attending church, I hope I've dispelled them. At least I know I've prepared you well as to how to handle them. Churches make requirements of attendees so easy even I can oblige. If there is some routine you don't get at first, there's a lot of freedom in knowing that the other attendees really don't care. (You know what I mean.)

CHAPTER SIX

I Don't Want to Sing, Raise My Hands or Jump Up and Down

I remember the first time I saw a person raise his hands in a church service. I thought someone had a gun in the guy's rib cage and was demanding his wallet.

When I realized he was worshipping God, I thought, *Holy Cow. What have we got going on here?* It made me uncomfortable. I don't know why. I've always been a hugger. I'll hug kids, women, other men and even my car when it gets me where I'm going with only fumes in the gas tank. But somehow seeing this fellow raise his hands to give God a hug hit me as odd. It was just such a free expression of his feelings for God, and I'd never seen it before.

Certainly, at that point in my journey toward God, I had not felt what that guy was feeling. I could tell his gesture was completely genuine, too—not something to show all of us who were not raising our hands how holy he was. To that guy, we weren't even in the room. On one hand, I found myself being critical of him. On the other hand, I was jealous. Both of my hands remained firmly clasped to the back of the pew in front of me.

That was almost twenty years ago. Now, after years of experiencing all the ways God expresses His love for me, I occasionally raise my hands in worship. I do it when I feel like doing it. It's between me and God—a hug of gratitude. I have no problem with people who don't raise their hands for whatever reason. How each person expresses himself to God is up to him. That's how it should be.

I tell you this to make it clear that you shouldn't avoid church because you don't want to sing, raise your hands or jump up and down. Even if other parishioners at the church you attend practice those expressions boldly and frequently, you shouldn't feel any responsibility to join in unless you want to. Maybe you're just a reserved person. That's a beautiful thing to be. Maybe you just don't want to fake feelings for God that you don't feel yet. That seems prudent to me. It's not like you are going to fool Him anyway. And who else matters?

Here's another example. Worship music touches me deeply. When I sing, I try to sing directly to God. Sometimes I get lucky and hit a right note. Sometimes it's a good thing everyone else is singing louder. How well I sing is not the point. I'm singing for Him.

But there are times when I don't sing with the congregation so I can listen. I could care less if anyone near me notices or is bothered that I'm not singing. I close my mouth and stay quiet for part of a song, a whole song or even for every song throughout a service. I'll tell you that during those times, I have had some of my most meaningful fellowship with God.

When my voice is silent, I can hear hundreds of other voices singing to Him. It can be so powerful to hear other flawed people—just like me—singing a love song to our God. And I'd swear I have heard Him singing back. If I sang just because I thought it was a requirement, I'd miss these moments. There is no such requirement. Sing when you want. Don't sing when you want.

If you're very concerned about the types of expression practiced at a particular church you're thinking of attending, find out before you go. In Part Three of this book, I offer suggestions about doing research to help identify a church that's potentially a good fit for you. Make sure worship style and worship practices are on your list of questions. Different Christian denominations participate in vastly different styles of worship. Even different churches within the same denomination can vary significantly.

While I've told you it's okay to participate at the level you want—no matter where you attend—that doesn't mean you can't try to find a church that has a style more like your own. There is no need to feel completely out of synch with the goings-on around you.

I'm now a longtime believer and church attendee, and I've found a church home that suits me. I don't feel at home in churches with very sedate worship. Nor do I feel at home in churches where parishioners are encouraged to express themselves however and whenever they want. I find that more distracting than uplifting.

There are fantastic Christian churches on both ends of the spectrum and everywhere in between. As I said in chapter 1, God isn't afraid of variety. For me, though, both ends of the worship style spectrum are wonderful places to visit, but I wouldn't want to live there. My home is somewhere in between. Likewise, you should be able to find a church that feels like home to you.

Chapter Seven

They Don't Want Someone Like Me There

Man. If there is a God, He wouldn't want to have anything to do with me until I clean up my act." That's a pretty common assumption for many of us until we finally get what God has been trying to tell us in His Word, which in my paraphrase goes something like this:

"Knucklehead! I know you're a mess! I already love you so much I let My own Son die on a cross in your place. He paid the price there for your mess already. It's done. You just have to accept it, accept Me. Tell Me you want Me as your Lord and Savior, and forgiveness is yours. Just come to Me as you are right now, and we'll work on your life together. But even that can wait until I throw a massive party in heaven. If you've ever had a messed-up kid come home to your love, you'd understand how I feel."

God's perspective is surprisingly different than we tend to assume it is because we know He hates sin—and He does—but He loves us. When He created people with free will, He gave us the freedom to choose to live in fellowship with Him or to walk away from Him into the darkness of our own decisions.

Here's the kicker: Every single one of us has walked away from Him into darkness. Every human being who ever walked the earth—except Jesus—has sinned.

Jesus was always God and never stopped being God. But He took on human flesh to experience every pain and temptation we do and to teach by example how to endure in God's light. Then, though He was absolutely sinless Himself, He was accused of a false charge, convicted and crucified on a cross. Why did God the Father let His own Son go through that? Because God loves you and wants you with Him.

You could never live perfectly as Christ did, so you could never be "good enough" to earn fellowship with Him and eternity in heaven. So He put all your sins, all my sins—all everyone's sins—on Jesus' back and let His blood wash them all away forever.

It was the most unselfish act of love ever performed in history. It was the greatest price anyone will ever pay for you. And even after that, God still gives us the choice to accept that payment for our own sins or to reject it. If we accept it, we are clean in His sight and welcome in His presence, even though we're still struggling to live rightly.

If you've never heard that before, it's a whopper of a revelation to drop on you in a little book about trying out church. I understand you may not believe it. But I do. I told you that to tell you this: Many of the people at any church you attend believe it. They don't see themselves as any better or any worse than you. They know that Jesus carried a huge pile of their sins on His back, too.

The people that truly get this, and that are truly humbled by it, know that they are every bit as flawed as you may feel right now. We've all sinned before, and we'll all sin again. We are all simply trying to get better every day to become worthy of the total forgiveness we received when we accepted Christ's gift of the cross. Just like the assumption in the opening quote of this chapter is wrong, so is thinking that the people in a Christian church wouldn't want you there.

You may encounter some hypocrites who present a holy air and give the impression that they disapprove of you. But you probably won't. I submit that those folks just don't get it, so don't worry about them if it happens.

In the Bible, Jesus tells a story about two men, a much-hated tax collector and a self-righteous religious leader, praying at the temple. The religious leader stands tall and prays loudly so all within shouting distance can benefit from his holiness. He says something along the lines of, "Thank

You, God, that I am so righteous and not like that awful tax collector over there. Thank You that I am so holy and good in all I do!" (I'm paraphrasing.)

In contrast, the lowly tax collector falls on his face in genuine repentance and humility, and cries out to God, "God, have mercy on me, a sinner." Jesus then tells His listeners that the tax collector is the one who has found favor with God, not the self-righteous man who put on a pious show.

Most of the people you'll encounter at church get this principle. (The ones who don't can be forgiven.) My point is to urge you to go to God—or at least go to church—just as you are, especially if the alternative is not to go at all. We're all a bunch of problem children trying to get better. Some of us have sinned really big. Others, perhaps, have sinned to lesser degrees. But all of us have fallen short of perfection and need God's forgiveness. We are all equally needy.

One of my best friends at church puts himself in the category of someone who sinned big and was forgiven big. He always tells a story that happened at our church before I started attending there. Apparently, at that time, it had come to the pastor's attention that our church was not particularly welcoming to someone who had "sinned big" and then began attending the church.

As my friend tells the story, the pastor interrupted his own sermon on a completely different topic and said, "It's come to my attention that someone visited this church and left feeling like we didn't want him here. Let me remind everyone here that we have all sinned and none of us deserve God's forgiveness, though many of us have received it by His grace. If you're visiting today, and you feel unwelcome, I want to know about it."

My friend said he wanted to cheer. He said that was the moment he knew he had found his church home. People who know they need God's forgiveness should always be ready to welcome others who seek it.

Be respectful of God and others when you go to church, even if you're not sure you believe the message. You are visiting a home with a family inside that loves it. Maybe someday you'll want to be part of the family. But you should never pretend to be perfect only because that's what you think the family expects. We want the real you there. So does He.

CHAPTER EIGHT

I Don't Know My Bible.
Heck, I Don't Even Have One

D id you know that if you ever go to one of those schools that teach you how to drive an 18-wheel tractor-trailer, they wouldn't expect you to drive up to the school in one on your first day? You're not expected to learn on your own before you go to where they teach you. It's the same with church. So don't worry if you don't "know your Bible." You're going to church to learn, and there's no test on the first day.

Church is a lot like that schoolhouse on the television show, *Little House on the Prairie*. All the grade levels were in the same room learning from the same teacher. The young ones weren't expected to know what the older ones knew. And the older ones sometimes helped the younger ones.

If you're going to church and hearing the Bible taught for the first time, you're a young one. You'll find at church that young ones come in every age, shape, educational background, race and economic position. So do the older ones, the students who are further along in their learning process.

Next time you feel like you should know your Bible better before sliding into church, remember that everyone else is there to learn their Bibles, too. It's understood that everyone is at a different place in the curriculum. It's also understood that no one is ever done learning God's Word. Some of its content is easy to grasp. Some of it takes time and meditation to fully comprehend. It's all too radical to be boring. It's all too meaningful to dismiss.

I'm not sure how you view the Bible right now. But if you begin to read it and hear it taught with the intention of learning, you'll never stop learning something new unless you choose to stop. Church is the perfect place to be if you genuinely want to learn.

I wouldn't worry too much if you don't have a Bible. Many churches have extras for attendees to borrow during services. It's also very common for a church to put the scriptures up on a big screen for everyone to see.

However, if you can afford a Bible, I highly recommend buying your own. Go to a Christian bookstore, let an employee know you're a beginner, and ask for a recommendation.

There are various translations that are widely accepted as accurate. I've used the New International Version (NIV) since I've been studying the Bible. The NIV is a modern translation that seems to be the standard used in teaching at most of the churches I've visited over the years.

It's still fairly formal English, but without all the "Thees" and "Thous" of the older King James Version. You'll be safe with an NIV. But there are others, so ask at the Christian bookstore for the pros and cons of each. Or, if you find a church before you buy a Bible, ask which version the church uses. Make sure to ask for a Bible that has both the Old Testament and the New Testament.

A good thing about having your own Bible is that you'll likely want to read it outside of church. Trust me. Even if you don't think you will, you probably will. I now have a Bible on my bedside table, another in my car, and another on my desk at work. I use every one of them at different times.

It's not that I'm all that holy. It's that I'm all that lazy and forgetful. If I had only one Bible, it'd be on my desk when I really needed it in my car. Or it'd be in my car when I needed it at my bedside. But you're not me. Unless they have a three-for-one sale at the Bible store, I'd say just get the one for now.

Another good thing about having your own Bible is that you can write in it. You can write notes from the pastor's sermon right next to the scripture he's teaching. You can also highlight passages that have special meaning so you can find them quickly. One of my wife's Bibles has so many things highlighted that I thought it had been printed on neon pink paper.

Her Bible—her rules; your Bible—your rules.

By the way, if you'd like to get a running start on your first church visit, there are a couple of things you can do. Read through the gospel of John. It's the fourth book of the New Testament and can be read in a couple of sittings. It's like an overview of the entire Bible in one book. It is the apostle John's writing on everything from creation, to Jesus' ministry on earth, to His death and resurrection.

Don't worry if you don't understand or believe everything it says. Remember, you're going to church to learn. The gospel of John will introduce you to the major topics that will be taught.

You might also find a local Christian radio station that features various Bible teachers. When I first started going to church, I found that radio Bible teachers helped me immensely as I tried to grasp what I was learning in church. I got in the habit of having my car radio tuned to the Christian stations most of the time.

The teachers became like friends since I listened to them so much. It's a habit I started in 1991 that's still going strong today. In fact, many of the same radio Bible teachers who were helping me then are still helping me now. Like I said, learning God's Word is an assignment you take on yourself, and you never graduate.

Do a little pre-church learning if you want a head start, or don't. Get yourself a Bible, or don't. You'll be welcome at church either way. We're all there to learn.

CHAPTER NINE

Sunday's My Day

My wife and I are both sports fanatics. We're the irritating kind of sports fanatics who actually schedule social activities around sporting events. I'm not just talking about the major sporting events that a lot of people schedule around. We schedule around evening replays of first rounds of PGA golf tournaments and regular season Major League Baseball games. It's a bit of a sickness. But we love it.

We're especially nuts about one NFL team. (I won't name the team lest I lose you as a reader over an opposing allegiance of your own.) When our team is scheduled to be on television, most people know not to even invite us over for anything at that time. They have learned that we'll either say no—or, worse, we'll show up, then sneak off to a television somewhere in the house and watch our team. (I already admitted it's a sickness. Let's move past that.)

Living on the West Coast, the early NFL games start at 10 on Sunday mornings, right smack-dab during church. My wife and I are often at the church until noon or so. We attend first service, then help out in the child care area during the second service every couple of weeks.

When our team is on early and we're scheduled to be at church until noon, it could be a great opportunity for us to take a day off from church. But we won't. Is it because we are so perfect and holy that we don't even feel the temptation to do so? No. It's that we made a firm decision long ago that Sunday is about worshipping God.

That decision, in advance, removed all the internal debating that we'd surely go through every Sunday our team is on television early. It's not even hard to do anymore because we've trained ourselves to commit to something—Someone—more than we commit to our own hobbies.

Don't get me wrong. We tend to scoot home a little faster from church on the days our team is on. But we have no conflict about which loyalty we serve first.

Perhaps you have a long tradition of Sunday being your day. It's your day to stay in bed until noon with the Sunday paper. It's your day to plant marigolds. It's your day to go golfing. It's your day to hang out at a sports bar and watch your team play.

Trust me, I know how hard a workweek can be, how busy a Saturday can be, and how enticing it is to have no commitments on a Sunday morning. I also know how much better it feels to spend Sunday morning with a church family, worshipping God and learning about His awesome love.

This is something you may not have experienced yet, so you may assume that there is no way church could be more uplifting than your own Sunday rituals. I'm asking you to take my word for it and give it a shot for a while. My wife and I still find plenty of time after church to watch sports. In fact, we've found that we enjoy our other Sunday activities so much more after beginning our day at church. I believe you will, too.

Remember that you're considering going to church because you're looking for some kind of difference in your life. It may be a major difference you're after, or a minor one. Wanting something is our motivation for trying anything new. Whether it's a new relationship, a new job, a new home or a new car, we're hoping for a new result of some kind.

If we don't try new things and open our minds to new possibilities, we're guaranteed not to have a new result. How we choose to spend our Sunday mornings is no different. If we are not willing to try church, we're guaranteed not to find out it offers the new results we're after.

The joy that often comes from other new experiences is temporary and external. It perks us up for a period of time, like a cup of strong coffee does. But the newness quickly wears off, and we find ourselves with the same old outlook on life we had before.

The joy that can come from experiencing the love of a church family and a living God is internal and eternal. It's something you will take with you wherever you go and whatever you do for the rest of your life—and beyond. It makes those other new experiences more meaningful and enjoyable. It can even make our appreciation of our existing relationships, jobs, homes and cars more complete.

Isn't what you have to gain worth a slight adjustment to your regular Sunday routine? (By the way, some Christian churches have services on Saturday. For the sake of simplicity, I'll keep talking about Sunday since it is the day of worship for most Christian churches.)

So far, I've been talking about the benefits to you and me of worshipping on Sunday. Did you know that there is a more important reason to worship on Sunday rather than do our own things? God deserves it. Throughout this book, I contend that church isn't the end. It's the means to an end. Church, without God, won't change your life much. Jesus Christ, the God that is taught about and worshipped at church, will.

If you're looking for new results in your life, experiencing God should be your goal. Even if you're unsure that He even exists, when you take the step of going to church, you can go with the hopes of finding that He does. And if this God does exist, and you're hoping He has something new for you, wouldn't it be wise to adjust your thinking from being primarily "you-centered" to being primarily "God-centered"?

If He really is God, He deserves our love, honor and worship. God is real. God is infinitely bigger than you and me. Yet He is intimately concerned with you and me individually. He already loves us. He desires that we love Him back. We show our love by seeking Him, by speaking with Him and by joining together with His other children to worship Him. This is why we go to church.

In this context, we realize that Sunday never really was "our day." It has always been His day, and we had been thinking just about ourselves when we thought it was ours.

Say you've got a wealthy uncle. He's always had a special spot in his heart for you, but you had better things to do than keep up your relationship with him. Maybe he hosts a family reunion every year, because he loves his extended family and loves to have them knitted together and part of his life.

Every year, he asks you to come to the reunion. He'll pay the airfare and the hotel bill if you'll just come. You know how much the reunion means to him and that having you there would make him the happiest man alive. After all, you're his favorite. It's the only thing he ever asks of you.

Yet, every year, you put him off and find something else you'd rather do. Then, one year, you have financial problems. He has all the resources to make your problems go away with a check he'd love to write. You call him and sheepishly ask for the money. He gives it gladly, without any guilt trip about the past.

Suddenly, you wish you had been as generous to him as he has always been with you. You wish you had been going to the reunions and calling your uncle more often in between. You wish you had thought of his feelings and his needs more than your own all those years. You don't feel this way because he laid on the guilt, but because he always deserved your consideration. All he wanted was your presence and your companionship. You could have given it, but you chose not to.

Have you been living out this same scenario with God? He wants you to come to His reunion. He wants to enjoy your companionship and for you to enjoy the companionship of the rest of the family. You need what He has to offer you from His abundant, limitless resources: forgiveness, help, strength, direction and love.

Be willing to give Him what He wants from you. If He is God, and if He will gladly give you what you need, doesn't He deserve a slight adjustment to your regular Sunday routine?

What if attending church on Sunday mornings means you have to give something up rather than simply pushing it back until you get home? There are only so many hours in a week. If you're a busy person with an activity-packed schedule, this could happen.

If your going to church and experiencing God is the one thing that can give you what all those activities cannot, wouldn't it be wise to give one of them up to find out?

Maybe you're a single mom with kids active in extracurricular activities all weekend long. Do you think you and your kids will be better off in one more dance class, or in church and Sunday school learning about the real purposes of your lives?

If you're a single man in five Fantasy Football leagues, do you think staying at home on Sunday morning to tally stats will add more value to your life than experiencing the power of a living God?

Remember, these are all activities that are fine in and of themselves. But they have never brought you closer to what you may be seeking. And they never will. If you want new results, be willing to invest your time in a new endeavor that might be able to provide them. If you must, be willing to let some of your old habits go to make room for some more productive new ones.

Trust a sports fanatic who remembers how great it was to stay in bed until noon with the Sunday paper and a big cup of coffee while watching his team on the tube. Indeed, that was a great way to spend Sunday mornings. But it doesn't compare with the immeasurable joy of the way I now spend my Sunday mornings. Not even close. I figured out that Sunday is His day. And that has made Sundays all the better.

CHAPTER TEN

They'll Want Me to Join Stuff

B y nature, I'm not a joiner. You know "joiners." Maybe you're one. These are folks that sign up for everything. God love 'em. Without them, nothing would get done. They're on the PTA committees. They organize your class reunions. They lead Girl Scout and Boy Scout groups. And they haven't missed a walk-a-thon for charity since they were eighteen. I really respect joiners because they are willing to invest their time and hearts in projects that benefit others. Most people, like me, are just happy someone else is doing it.

Now if you were to see the various activities I'm involved with today, you might think I am a joiner by nature. I'd say it's more like I'm becoming a joiner despite my nature. A few years back, I identified that my powerful capacity to say no and sit on the sidelines was not a good trait. If I truly believe in helping people—and I do—then why wouldn't I invest myself in them? Being self-centered and stingy with God was the only honest answer I could come up with. I didn't like that answer, so I decided to change it.

Since then, I've tried to change my default "no" setting to a positive response and get in the game more often. Through my church and other affiliations, if I don't have a decent reason to say no, I try not to. I have to admit, I wish I'd started earlier. I find that I enjoy helping when I can. I like the relationships I've formed since jumping in with various project squads. But regardless of how many projects I get involved with these days, it's still not a natural response for me. When you're not a joiner by nature, it doesn't change overnight. At least I'm working on it.

Church has no shortage of activities that need joiners: organizers, mission workers, gofers, set-up crews, breakdown crews, childcare volunteers, donators, bakers, casserole experts, drivers, teachers, and check-in table attendees. I'm actually proud of the Christian church for that. It means the church is engaged and trying to make a difference in people's lives.

Unfortunately, though, churches are so legendary for needing joiners that some people don't want to start going to church for fear they'll get the full-court press. Even natural joiners can have this barrier to attending church because they only want to join efforts they feel good about. If church is a new experience for them, they don't know if they feel good about it going in.

Of course, it's even more intimidating to people who are thinking about going to church for the first time and who are not natural joiners. When I first started going to church I had this concern. I admit that I kept my head low for a while, assuming that if I looked up, I'd be pressed into something I didn't want to join. It never happened.

If you'd like to try attending church but have stayed away because you don't want to get recruited to help with "extra-churchular" activities, you're my kind of person. While I cannot promise that you won't be asked, I can promise that you are allowed to say no without retribution or public embarrassment. It's that simple. If someone asks you to help with a church activity, and you just don't want to do it, say no. It's okay. The askers hear no all the time. They even have to say no themselves sometimes. It's no big deal.

Remember, your primary reasons for going to church are to learn about God, to worship Him and to enjoy the fellowship of other worshippers. You're not there to impress or appease fellow worshippers. And most would rather you politely say no to a request than to realize you only said yes because you felt pressured. Or, worse yet, you say yes, then bail out at the last minute when they cannot replace you.

Attending church services on Sunday might be enough for you for a while as you explore and learn. However, if and when you are ready, you might derive tremendous satisfaction from getting involved.

In church services, you rarely have a chance to get to know your fellow worshippers. Even though you may enjoy attending services, you might not feel connected while you're in the "service only" mode. You'll likely look around and see so many others who seem to know and enjoy each other. Remember, they all started just like you at one point. After they got acclimated, they wanted to participate with others at a teamwork level. They joined in here and there, and quickly made friends.

I hope you reach the point where you want to contribute to your church's activities. Becoming involved in extra activities will get you into more personal contact with wonderful people like you who are just trying to help others. In these settings, you'll begin to find friendships rather than just pew-mates. You'll get to know people and begin to feel like you "belong" rather than simply "attend." It will also give others a chance to get to know you and care about you as a person. Until you're ready, though, you're perfectly welcome to attend services and leave the joining to others.

CHAPTER ELEVEN

I'm Not Even Sure
I'm Buying What They're Selling

Here you are just a nice, normal person who has some interest in trying out church for whatever reason, and I'm laying some pretty heavy ideas on you. You might be thinking, *Discovering a personal relationship with the true living God? What's that about? I just want to find some tips on how to be a better person. Maybe go to a church picnic and meet some people.*

Let me assure you that if all you want are some life lessons and pleasant social activities, you'll likely find those things at a good Christian church. But those things will not be the central focus of the teaching at a good Christian church. It's the "heavy ideas" I've shared throughout these pages that are the church's reason for being, even if they are not your reason for being there.

It's something you might like to know before arriving at church for your trial run. My whole purpose for writing this book is to pass along the inside information I wish a regular churchgoer would have shared with me before I began going to church.

While I'm encouraging you to take the step you have already begun to consider, I'm not trying to do it under false pretenses. I'm giving you the lowdown and the what-for to help you go into it prepared. Whether it makes you more eager or more apprehensive, you need to know that a good Christian church will teach that Jesus is the living God, that He cares about you personally, that faith in Him will guarantee you a place in heaven, and that the Bible is the inspired Word of God.

It's okay if you don't believe those things now. Obviously, I believe they are eternally important to believe at some point before you leave this earth. Since none of us knows when that'll be, I'd say "the sooner the better" is an understatement. "Now" would be even better, since we need God's help while we're here on earth, too.

But this book is about honesty and reality. The reality is that you're only considering going to church, perhaps for the first time as a potential regular attendee, and you might not believe any of these wonderful and radical concepts at this moment. Perhaps you've never even heard these ideas stated as directly as I've stated them.

If I've made you feel a bit confronted on these important spiritual principles, be prepared that you'll likely experience that feeling at church as well. Sure, you'll get a warm, fuzzy sermon and an invitation to a potluck once in a while. But I'd be disappointed if that's all you get out of church.

You, like many others, might be holding back on attending church because you're not sure you're in the market for that deep spiritual stuff. Let me ask you a personal question: What are you afraid of?

If you start going to church to find the things you're in the market for—life pointers, meeting nice people, etc.—and you find those things, you're ahead. When fundamental Christian principles are taught, you're allowed to ignore them or write them off as fiction. It's your choice. The church isn't selling you anything. And neither am I. We both want you to have the truth and make your own decision with good information. You'll hear the truth at a good Christian church. The rest is up to you.

CHAPTER TWELVE

They'll Tell Me Not To Do All the Things I Like Doing

Do you have the impression that Christianity and the church are anti-fun? I admit that before I started going to church regularly, I thought I was going to be surrounded by boring prudes who never smiled. I figured the main job of a pastor was to remind the congregation each week of everything fun they weren't allowed to do.

I went to church anyway because I was looking for meaning in my life, and I wanted to learn about this Jesus I'd been avoiding. I just figured enduring a little uptight boredom came with the package.

Can I tell you what I found at church? I found the funniest, most interesting, most outrageously colorful people I've ever met in my life. And most of them seemed authentic and genuinely happy. These were good people there to learn about Jesus just like me. They had flaws, triumphs, defeats, problems and questions. And getting to know them was a blast. Sure, I ran into a sourpuss once in a while. But I discovered that the sourpusses were a tiny minority, and the fun ones were all over the place. I could feel comfortable being me.

Before you think I'm making all this up, let me remind you that I'm not on commission. I really am not trying to sugarcoat anything to dupe you into going to church. Every word is the truth as I've experienced it.

I must say that different churches I've visited do have different atmospheres. There have been some that are more somber than others. Even those more sedate churches never left me with the impression that good Christians should be sourpusses. They were just less outwardly jovial than other churches. That appeals to some people, and I'm glad those churches are there for them.

The three churches I've called home in my Christian walk, however, have all been filled with laughter. Maybe that's why God led me to them. I'm glad these churches have been there for people like me. I believe that if you follow the simple research steps I suggest in Part Three of this book, you'll be able to find a church that feels like home to you.

Let's talk a little bit about that list of things you're pretty sure the church will tell you are off-limits for Christians. It does exist. (See, I told you I wasn't into false advertising.) There absolutely are things that a good Christian church will teach against because God teaches against them in His Word.

Reading the Ten Commandments in Exodus, one of the books near the beginning of the Bible, will give you a good overview. The specific "thou shalts" and "thou shalt nots" all sort of flow out of these Commandments. If you're into worshipping anything more than you worship God, that's a don't. Showing love to your neighbor—any other traveler on life's road who needs your help—is a do. Taking that too far and lusting after your neighbor's wife, big don't. Take a moment to crack open your Bible (Exodus, chapter 20) or go online to read the Ten Commandments. I'll wait.

Any church that teaches that doing the "thou shalt nots" or not doing the "thou shalts" is okay is not a good Christian church. If we're living contrary to those directives that came directly from God—and we all have in one way or another—a good Christian church has the responsibility to help us by recommending that we change how we're living.

I'll bring you back to my assumption that you're reading this book because you're looking for better results in life, and you're open to the prospect that a Christian church can help you toward that goal. Are you willing to make any changes in your life to change your results? If you have every intention of doing things your own way, even when you learn that God has a better way, you really cannot expect church to do much for you.

God didn't lay these principles on us to take away our fun. He gave them to us because He created us and He knows what real joy is. He knows our propensity for seeking destructive, short-term "fun" that derails us from true eternal joy He wants us to experience. His Commandments point us to better, more productive, more satisfying life results.

The chief engineer who oversaw the design of the car you drive put great care into every detail. That baby is designed to provide comfort, reliability and performance. The designer wanted you to enjoy your car for many years. So he, knowing its inner workings down to the smallest part, provided a manual. If you follow the recommendations in that manual, your car will deliver comfort, reliability and performance for many years.

If you don't do the things the manual recommends, or you do things the manual advises against, your car won't deliver on its potential. That's your right and your decision. But don't get mad at the designer for telling you how his design was intended to work at its peak. And certainly don't blame the designer when your car breaks down because you chose to ignore the manual.

The Bible is the Designer's manual to teach us how to get the peak performance out of ourselves. We might prefer to ignore His instruction when it contradicts how we want to live. That is our nature. We will, however, live a better life and a blessed eternity if we change our driving habits to conform to His manual.

There is something that might surprise you about Christianity, though. It is really more about freedom than it is about restriction. You might assume that some of the things you love to do are expressly forbidden as sin by God, but they aren't. God created many of the pleasures we enjoy in this life for a very important reason: He wants us to enjoy them!

I won't go through a list of freedoms you do or don't have when you become a follower of Christ. It will get us away from the focus of this book, and different Christian denominations teach differently about some of these things. Some may teach that enjoying a glass of wine with a meal is absolutely fine. Others may teach that letting any alcohol touch your lips is sinful. Hopefully, all would teach that drinking to the point of drunk-enness or encouraging a friend with an alcohol problem to drink is clearly not God's will for us. This is just one example, and we'll end it there.

The key thing for you to take away is that not everything enjoyable is a sin. Rather than avoiding church on the assumption it'll be a downer and mess up all your fun, check it out. You might be pleasantly surprised. I was.

CHAPTER THIRTEEN

You Can Still Believe in God Without Going to Church

There are many people who say that you don't have to go to church to worship God. I agree. There are some true followers of Christ who are unable to go to church but are every bit as Christian as regular churchgoers. Perhaps they are housebound for some reason and simply cannot get to church. Or they live in one of the many countries where it's a crime to confess Christ and to assemble in His name. There simply are no churches to attend. Or perhaps these believers are in jail for breaking this law and meeting in a secret home church that was discovered. These are Christians who are dearly loved by Christ, the object of their faith.

There is something that most of these believers have in common. They would love the opportunity to attend church regularly and without persecution. If they could get free of their sickbeds, their isolation and their jail cells to get to Bible-teaching churches, they would be the first ones there. They would not just attend on Sundays as some kind of commitment to cross off their to-do lists for the week.

It would be a privilege and a gift they would cherish. Why? Because they understand the importance of being instructed in God's Word and in the joining together of the church to worship as one body. This concept is so clearly taught throughout the Bible that anyone choosing to follow Christ should desire to attend church.

If you ever hear someone who professes to be a Christian and who is perfectly able to go to church say, "I'm a Christian, but I choose not to go to church," I'd say you're hearing a Christian who is choosing not to follow God's teaching. That person's reasons almost don't matter. Maybe he's truly a saved believer who took personal offense at something someone did or said at church, and avoiding church altogether is his way of dealing with it.

Maybe he prefers to do other things on Sundays and is using his Christian freedom to rationalize his choices. I contend that he is choosing to keep himself from God's best for his life, and his Christian walk will suffer at some point. There is another possibility. The professed Christian who simply chooses not to go to church may not be a Christian. He might like the title, but he is showing by his choices that he values other things more than he values his life with Christ and Christ's followers. Only God knows that person's heart.

I give you this example because you may not be a Christian. You're simply considering the possibility of attending a Christian church to discover some things about God and yourself. I applaud you for looking for answers where I believe you may truly find them.

But maybe you've heard someone present a convincing argument that you don't need to go to church to find or worship God. Let me say that I believe whoever told you that is only trying to make himself feel better about his own choices. Worse, he is trying to take you down with him. Don't let him.

The fact that you're even considering looking for something of value at a Christian church means that you haven't found it elsewhere. Maybe you've even thought it, yourself: *If God is real, I shouldn't have to go to church to find Him.* Let me ask you, how has that been working out for you so far?

God created us to be a part of His family, the church. He designed the church to work like a human body. He's the head—the brain (control central), if you will. Maybe I'm an arm and you're a hand. A hand that isn't connected to the arm isn't helping the arm reach its full potential. Likewise, the arm can't take a hand that isn't connected where it needs to go. But when that hand is connected to the arm, and the arm is connected to the body, and the body is connected to the head, all the parts of the body can help each other. Each part of the body is better for it. The entire body is better for it. Church is where the body gets connected. If you want your life to reach its highest potential, stay connected.

Attending church on Sundays to stay connected to the body is critically important. And it's just the beginning. I've already told you that I believe God is far too concerned with the intimate details of our lives to make Himself available to us only from 9 until noon on Sundays.

Of course, I believe that people can and should worship God when they're not in church. In fact, it's during the struggles and challenges of daily life outside the protective atmosphere of church where we need Him most! Just getting a charge on Sunday mornings won't change your life. Staying connected to the power source, God and the church body, all throughout your week is where the real juice is.

There are a lot of ways to stay connected. You can have your own daily quiet time to read the Bible and pray. You can listen to Christian radio to learn the Bible and to hear uplifting worship music. If you do any of these things in the car—which I highly recommend—make sure you keep your eyes open no matter how much you get into it. (Don't ask how I learned this. Just trust me.)

You can attend other classes or get-togethers your church offers during the week. I attend a men's Bible study on Friday mornings at my church. The men who sit at my table have become irreplaceable friends to me. These are regular guys just like me. We challenge each other in our learning and our faith. We can call each other any time we need anything— a sounding board on a business or family matter, help with a project, someone to pray for us in a difficult time—anything. They'd do any of those things for me.

If I get off track, they lovingly hold me accountable to do the right thing. Wouldn't you like to have more of those positive friendships in your life? Do you think that staying connected on Sundays and all through the week would lead you closer to or further away from a better life?

I'm not saying you have to do all of these or you won't get anything out of going to church on Sundays. Maybe you'll want to do these things after you've attended church for a while. I just want you to understand that going to a good Christian church is important if you want to experience God and learn about Him. I'd say it's the minimum commitment you should make if you want those things. Church is not an obligation to suffer through or to avoid if at all possible. It's a gift God wants to give you so you can be connected to His family, His body.

My pastor points to the construction of the cross as a visual reminder of this point. The cross has one vertical beam of wood that reminds us of our connection to Christ who is above us. The cross also has a horizontal beam of wood that reminds us of our connection to our brothers and sisters to the left and right of us. What Christ went through on the cross reminds us how important both of those relationships are to Him.

Finally, worshipping God should not even really be about what you want. It should be about what God wants. Worshipping God is doing things that are important to Him to show our love and gratitude. He has clearly said in His Word—take my word for it if you haven't read it—that the joining together of His followers is important to Him. Take the step. Go to church. Try worshipping Him on His terms: in church on Sundays and outside of church all week long. Worshipping on your terms really isn't worship.

CHAPTER FOURTEEN

Church Is for Weak-Minded People

I f something is true and truly good for you, is it weak-minded to do it? If you are about to drown and someone tosses you a rope to pull you to safety, is it weak-minded to grab the rope? If you're drowning in a negative spiral of life and someone encourages you to grab onto the one thing that got him out of a negative spiral of life, is it weak-minded to explore his suggestion?

Whenever I hear someone attempt to justify why he doesn't go to church by saying religion and church are crutches for the weak, I agree with him. Then I ask, "What's wrong with a crutch if it's real and what you need?" When you've got a broken leg, it's perfectly acceptable to use a crutch. I wouldn't suggest using an imaginary one. You'll just tip over and hurt yourself even worse. Using a real crutch, made of sturdy wood or metal, is a pretty darn intelligent thing to do. It keeps you upright and allows you to keep moving forward while you're healing.

We're all broken in some way or another. You, me, and the guy who justifies avoiding church by saying it's for weak-minded people, are all damaged goods. Whether great or small, our injuries are real.

It takes great strength of mind to admit that we need help and seek true healing. It doesn't matter if we have been told we should be able to heal ourselves or that we think people will consider us weak for needing help. The ones who get healthy are the ones who accept help.

Getting healthy with help is far better than continuing to try to heal ourselves and continuing to fail. We go to a medical doctor for bodily ailments. Church is the best place to turn to when our hurt is something other than a physical disorder.

Billions of broken people throughout the ages—many far more strong-minded than you or me—have sought true, eternal help from the same source and received healing. Their source was—and still is—the God of the Bible. They were smart enough to want truth rather than the world's false promises, forgiveness rather than the world's condemnation, and a relationship with Jesus rather than acceptance by the world's cynics. Please don't think that they were all wrong, delusional or unintelligent. They were—and are—the smart ones. I'm happy to be associated with them. It makes me a smart one, too.

There was a time I considered myself to be far too intelligent and self-sufficient to rely on God. This was quite ironic, because I'd sure get mad at Him if things weren't going my way. I might even start making deals with Him if I was really scared and wanted Him to come to my rescue. I believed He was real and that He was a lot bigger than me.

But still I thought His real followers were weak. I mean, these people actually went to church and tried to live their lives by God's rules. Weak. In retrospect, I think I knew they were right all along. I seem to recall that I envied them, too. So I had to come up with some reason to convince myself I was justified in not joining them.

Consequently, I used to be the guy who said church was a crutch for the weak. Imagine that. I believed in God and called His followers weak. I am my own best case study that calling Christian churchgoers weak-minded was, in itself, weak-minded. It would have made more sense if I just flat didn't believe in God. Then I would have had a more intelligent premise on which to label His followers weak-minded.

If God wasn't real—if He was just an imaginary crutch—I'd be the first to tell you to look somewhere else for support. If, after 18 or so years of going to church and studying His Word, I had honestly found no evidence that He is real, I'd be writing books declaring the hoax. That would probably be an easier gig.

I'd be a hit on the talk-show circuit. For sure, I'd be watching football in bed on Sunday mornings rather than looking forward to going to church. My relationship with Jesus is the best thing that ever happened to me. But I wouldn't give Him the time of day if I were not certain He is who He said He is in His Word.

I've got to be honest, He cramps my style sometimes. He compels me to be generous when I want to be stingy. When I want to lay a little righteous indignation on someone for doing me wrong, He thumps me on the head and reminds me of all the wrongs for which He's forgiven me. If that doesn't take the fun out of making someone else squirm, I don't what would. If He hadn't used church to show Himself to me, I'd have no incentive to go. And I would not be attempting to help you along the same path I walked.

I am neither a theologian nor a rocket scientist. However, I am a reasonably intelligent person. If we were to meet in a business setting, you'd probably think I was very normal with flashes of mental sharpness. If you learned I was a churchgoing Christian, I doubt you'd think it was because I couldn't think for myself.

It's precisely the opposite. I can and do think for myself. When I am presented with a choice, I'll choose the option that makes more logical *and* emotional sense to me. I'll stick with it if I know it's right—even if it's not the popular or politically correct option. I might change my mind if someone presents better evidence to the contrary. But if his best argument is that he thinks I'm weak-minded because I think differently than he does, I can live with him thinking I'm weak-minded. I know the truth about myself.

If my own perceptions about myself don't convince you that church and Christianity are not just for weak-minded folks, consider this: Some of the most intelligent people in the world became Christians after setting out to prove Christianity was false. These are people who had ironclad IQs and worldly reputations on the line. Some were devout atheists whose mission in life was to convince others to join them. They set out to present evidence that Christianity was a myth and found themselves convinced it was true. Ooops.

Check out people like atheist-turned-Christian Lee Strobel, who after a nearly two-year investigation of the evidence for Jesus, received Christ into his heart in 1981 and has become a leading apologist for faith in Jesus Christ. He is the former award-winning legal editor of *The Chicago Tribune* and is a *New York Times* best-selling author of nearly twenty books, including *The Case for Christ, The Case for Faith, The Case for a Creator*, and *Inside the Mind of Unchurched Harry and Mary*.

You might find it interesting to do a little research on your own. A brief search online, at a Christian bookstore or at a local library will likely convince you that smarter people than you and me—and the guy who says Christian church is for the weak-minded—discovered that Jesus is who He said He is.

Next time someone tries to tell you church or Christianity is for the weak-minded, remember people like Lee Strobel. At this point in your life, you may not have discovered for yourself that Christianity is true. But the strong-minded thing to do would be to at least consider that the strong-minded people who have accepted Christ could be right. Consider that I could be right. Church is not for the weak-minded. Church is for people who are willing to hear the evidence and decide for themselves what is true and what is not.

Chapter Fifteen

Organized Religion Is About Men, Not God

Of all the justifications not to go to church, the argument that the Bible and religion were created by men is a powerful one. Why? Well, because in a way, it's true. Let me handle them separately, starting with the Bible.

I remember two distinct conversations I had with Bible believers before I was one of them. Each tried to convince me of something by telling me it was in the Bible. Of course, because it was in the Bible made it "fact" and true to them. But at the time, just because something was in the Bible meant nothing to me.

I remember how smug I was in reply: "The Bible was written by flawed men. Why would you believe something to be true just because some guy wrote it?" From the vantage point of my high horse, I remember almost pitying both of these Bible believers. I was bitter and accusatory in my delivery, which even then was very unlike me. I had a way of getting along with everybody and typically found ways to be pleasant with people, even when I disagreed with them.

But I did not extend this courtesy to these two people. Neither of them was rude to me in our discussion. Yet my response was to slam the Bible—a book that was very precious to them for some reason I had not yet discovered.

Do you know why I lashed out rudely? Because I was a dog backed into a corner. I did not want to believe the Bible was the accurate revelation of God because that would mean I'd have to change. I didn't want to change. I wanted to live how I wanted to live—regardless of the darkness

I felt. I believed in God, but I wanted Him to deliver on my demands and otherwise stay out of my business.

If I started to believe the Bible was true, that would mess up everything—and I knew it. How dare they make me consider the possibility? So without hearing them out and never having read the Bible or hearing it taught in depth, I cut them off with disdain. There are two reasons I will never forget these two instances. One is that I am profoundly sorry. The other is that I have been profoundly changed. Now I know that the Bible is the accurate revelation of God to men.

Two things about my response to them were true: The books of the Bible were physically penned by men, and the writers all had flaws. Some of them had major flaws. They were, indeed, human. But that's all I was right about. After years of reading, studying, listening to teaching and allowing God to open my mind to the Bible, I can come to no other conclusion than to believe that it is the Word of God.

Jesus is who He said He is in His Word. If you are truly curious and want to investigate this further for yourself, there are wonderfully written and compelling books on the subject. Let me give you just a few reasons to consider that belief in the divine imprint on the Bible is based on far more than blind faith:

- The Bible is comprised of 66 books written over thousands of years by men with no opportunity to consult one another. Yet there are no contradictions.
- Many specific Old Testament prophesies about the coming Messiah, written thousands of years before Jesus Christ, were all fulfilled in the life of one man, Jesus Christ. Good guessing or some well-orchestrated hoax could not account for this level of detailed accuracy.
- Most of the authors of the New Testament, the disciples who walked with Christ, were killed for their faith. They could have easily gotten off the hook if they had admitted it was a carefully

crafted hoax. The apostle Paul—who did not walk with Christ, but rather persecuted Christians before God revealed Himself to him—had every reason to debunk Christianity as heresy. Yet he spent the remainder of his life after his conversion writing a good portion of the New Testament. Much of that time, he was in prison for his beliefs.

Personally, I think that divine inspiration is even more plausible because the men who wrote the scriptures were flawed and admitted it. It would be like me, someone who is mathematically challenged, plotting out the equation for Einstein's Theory of Relativity before he did, and getting it right. I could never do that on my own. It would have to be divine inspiration.

Take it a step further and say someone was holding a gun to my head telling me to call it a hoax or die. If it was a hoax, you can bet I'd sing like a canary. But if I knew it was the hand of God that led me, I'd fear God more than the bullet.

Just these few observations should suggest a very real possibility that the words in the Bible, though physically written by mere men, were given to these men by the Spirit of God. My goal here is not to convince you outright that the Bible is the infallible Word of God. Rather I hope to simply open your mind with logic that it could very well be.

If you have avoided church because you, like I once did, assume or even hope the Bible isn't the authentic Word of God, I hope you reconsider. Investigate the Bible on your own and through its teaching at church. For myself, I can tell you that discovering its veracity was not the downer I thought it would be. It has brought so much joy and clarity to my life. It sustains me and gives me hope where I once had only fear and uncertainty. Even now, though I struggle with sin, selfish pride, negativity and life's challenges, I have an underlying certainty that Christ loves me and that I'll spend eternity with Him in heaven. He said it in His Word. I know it.

Now let's look at religion. Religion is a loaded word with various connotations. There are many "religions" declaring different gods or life paths. If we call the Christian faith a religion, we mean that it has structure or guidelines and a unity of beliefs as do other religions. But a great difference between the Christian religion and other religions is that Christianity does not require being "religious" to attain salvation and eternity with the Creator.

Christianity is the one religion in which the Creator, knowing we are incapable of sustained religious perfection, came to earth in bodily form to become perfection for us. He, the Christ, lived the perfect life we never could. Then He paid the humiliating, bloody price for our imperfections on the cross. His only requirement for us is to accept what He did for us so His payment could be applied to our accounts.

If we truly do this, our gratitude and freedom will compel us to want to please Him and become more like Him every day. The good deeds we choose to do will come from our hearts as evidence of our faith in what He did for us, not to earn His favor or acceptance. We will still sin, stumble and struggle against our imperfect flesh. But the Father will see us as clean because of our faith in His Son, Jesus. For His followers, Jesus' payment covers all sins—past, present and future. His forgiveness is the only way a broken, sinful person like me could ever hope to have fellowship with a holy God.

This is a marked contrast to other religions, which all require that their followers "do" religious things to earn God's approval. This means that they hope God uses a scale system and that by doing more good things than bad things, one earns salvation. But God is perfect, or He wouldn't be God. Why would anyone assume they could be good enough to earn His favor?

More impossible still is that any human, other than Jesus, could live a perfect life from birth to death. Our rebellious nature is so much a part of us that it rears its head almost as soon as we're born. Any religion that requires earning or deserving fellowship with God leaves man on one side of a great canyon and God on the other with no bridge between them.

Christ is the bridge we can all cross because it is built on His perfection, His payment on the cross, His desire to save us and His divinity—not ours.

This is the huge difference between the religion of Christianity and all other religions. If we talk about the Christian religion as the institution of the church, it is much like the Bible. It may involve human hands and efforts, but it is the result of divine inspiration.

The church—the collective body of believers in Christ, past, present and future—is called the bride of Christ. He loves the church, provides for His church and directs His church as He will. He prepares a place for His church in heaven. The Christian church was not created by men to gain control over other men. It was created by Christ to be His bride. He delights in His bride.

In the church, like in all good things Christ has given us, we humans sometimes get in the way and pervert what is good. As long as the church is on earth and is made up of humans, the church will be imperfect.

There are many examples in history of men trying to use the church for their own purposes. Sadly, there is no denying this. But these perversions of God's intentions for the church are detestable to God, defilements of His bride.

God will always deal harshly with those who pervert His church. But those who love His church—leaders and laypeople alike—will enjoy God's blessings. He knows the hearts of those who don't love Him, no matter how "religiously" they present themselves outwardly. He also knows the hearts of those who truly are His followers, no matter how imperfect they are.

If you've avoided being a part of God's church because you believe it was created by misdirected men for misdirected purposes, then you've let misdirected men rob you of too much. You have believed a lie. Or, worse, you chose to believe the lie so you would have an excuse not to change. I speak from experience on this topic.

I again come back to the fact that you're probably reading this book because you seek some change. To receive it, you'll have to get past all the lies you've believed, the misperceptions you've had, and the excuses you've used to justify not changing. I remember that this was a hard step for me to take. I did it anyway because I felt the pull of something I did not understand. I just knew it was time to stop hiding and see for myself.

Are you ready to stop hiding and see for yourself?

PART TWO

One Great Reason
You Should Go to Church

CHAPTER SIXTEEN

God Uses Churches—
Even Imperfect Ones—to Bless People

This is where I ask you to believe that one is greater than fifteen. We've completed fifteen chapters, each presenting a good reason not to go to church. Hopefully, I've given you new ways of thinking about those fifteen reasons. However, I understand my words alone might not be enough to convince you that I'm right. So I'd like you to consider that there is one great reason to go to church that trumps all 15 reasons not to: *God uses imperfect churches, filled with imperfect people, to bless people.*

For whatever reason, you're at least considering attending a Christian church. Even if you're not entirely sure why, there is something inside you that wonders—even hopes—that you or your family might have something to gain. Maybe you want to learn more about Christ, as I did.

Maybe you've made a terrible mess of life, and you'd like help to turn yourself around from the inside out. Maybe life, through no fault of your own, has made a terrible mess of you, and you'd like to find hope and friendship. It may be as simple as wanting your kids to have some positive influences and moral training on Sunday mornings.

You're not sure if church is the answer, but you're sure the other things you've tried in the past have not been the answer. Perhaps you're even open to the wonderful idea that what you seek is about more than going to church. There might really be a loving God who wants to forgive you, help you, save you. Let me fuel the hope: There is. And a Christian church can help you discover Him.

In no way is the God of the Bible limited to special appearance on

Sundays within the walls of church buildings. Not even close. In fact, if you accept God, His Holy Spirit will dwell inside you wherever you are. But attending a good Christian church is a much better way of discovering Him than taking your chances on your own.

At the very least, you've given other things a try, and they haven't quite worked out. You may have found some things that take your mind off your questions or problems for a while. Television, movies, parties, work, working out and gardening can be nice distractions. But they haven't given you a clearer understanding of your purpose in life. And they surely haven't suggested God's purpose for your life.

I'm not against enjoying any of those things. However, I will tell you that they will never provide what you likely are seeking. I've been there, done that, and found something more meaningful in the highest degree.

I was every bit as skeptical, self-sufficient and confused as you may be right now. The difference came when I was willing to at least try a Christian church. Did I find imperfect people there? Sure. Did I understand or agree with everything right away? No. But, eventually, I realized an incredible, unexpected blessing because I went.

God used church and imperfect people to reach me, love me and help me get on a better road for my life. I found wonderful, caring friends and mentors who have added so much more to my life than anything I've ever been able to do for them. I am confident that participating in a good Christian church will do the same for you—so sure that I urge you to take the first step.

To say that I've never had a problem since attending church and finding God would be a lie. Don't believe people who try to sell you on church by saying all your problems will be solved magically and immediately. You'll only be setting yourself up for disenchantment. God promises to be with us *in* our troubles. He does not promise that we won't have them.

As I've said, we're works-in-progress even after God enters our lives. Imagine that you're a block of marble in the hands of a great sculptor. He uses blessing and difficulties to carve and shape you into the perfect work of art He sees in His mind the whole time. The process can be exhilarating and painful at times. But, if you put yourself in the hands of the Master, you will become what He envisions.

Okay, that was an important disclaimer to make sure you don't go to church one time and feel cheated because you're still behind on your bills the next day. Now here's the flip side. God can and does intervene quickly and miraculously in the lives of His kids—sometimes.

Sometimes it's tangible and direct. You're struggling with drugs and He miraculously takes away your desire to do drugs. Your wayward spouse has a change of heart and asks for your forgiveness. Or God opens your heart to a true message of hope and acceptance to give you strength to fight life's negative pulls.

In other words, you might go to church once and experience something supernatural. Those decisions are God's alone. But He may be waiting for you to seek, ask and accept what He has for you. A Christian church is a wonderful place to seek and ask.

If God does want to touch your life through a church family—and I guarantee you He does—there is one sure-fire way to not receive that touch: Simply stay away from church, the imperfect people there and the teaching of the Bible. You can keep on trying all the other things you've been trying—all to no avail. God will keep on grieving like the loving father He is—a father who desires to help a suffering child, even the one who isn't interested in His help.

So why don't you at least take a step to find out? What do you have to lose by seeing if what I say is true? The possibility of what you have to gain outweighs the alternatives. If you're in a desert dying of thirst and someone tells you there is cool, fresh water just over the next sand dune, isn't it worth a look? I've been over the next sand dune and tasted the water. Trust me, it's worth a look.

A Christian church is not the water. It will simply point you to the water—a real and loving God. You'll find encouragement on your journey from other travelers who are no better or worse than you. And experiencing God is something far better than just experiencing a nice church service. He will change your life in ways that substitutes can't—if you let Him.

PART THREE

Checking Out Christian Churches
One Step at a Time

CHAPTER SEVENTEEN

Use Your Skepticism as a Tool

Perhaps I've encouraged you to get past the fifteen good reasons not to go to church—or any others you have that I didn't cover—and to look into the one great reason to go.

Don't worry if you're still skeptical. It's an honest reaction to trying something new. Don't let your skepticism keep you from trying something that could provide what you seek. Rather, be honest with yourself about your skepticism, as well as with anyone who asks as you take your first steps. Use your skepticism to get answers to questions, to avoid situations for which you don't feel ready, and to say no to requests you're not ready to fulfill.

It's a very sane thing to want to tiptoe into new waters. Not everyone likes to dive headfirst into uncertain conditions. Maybe the water's cold, and you prefer getting acclimated slowly. Maybe you want to make sure the water is deep enough before you do a high dive off the tallest platform. Likewise, "carefully" is a perfectly fine way to explore church.

One thing to consider, however, is that you're seeking something new and different for your life. So, while skepticism isn't bad, don't let it close your mind to new and different ways of looking at life. If you hold so tightly to your skepticism that there is no possibility you'll accept anything church has to offer, what's the point?

It's like embarking on a new dating relationship. Maybe you've been hurt or embarrassed in a relationship that ended badly. You can say you want to find a new meaningful relationship. But if all you bring to the next relationship is forty-foot brick walls and bitterness, are you really giving a new relationship a chance of being meaningful?

You have to be willing to be open, to be hopeful and to be changed. You have to be willing to take a risk and open your mind to new ways of thinking, especially if it's new results you're after. It's the only way you can get what you say you want.

Decide now to move forward in your exploration of Christian church, being honest about your skepticism, but completely open that attending church could be a positive step toward finding what you're seeking. If you can do that, then the rest of this book will be valuable to you. It provides useful tips on how to wade into the water gently.

Some ideas may be common sense. But others could very well be steps you never thought of, offered by a friend who knows the ropes and who once shared your skepticism. Think of it as getting trained for a new job in a safe environment before any customers or coworkers show up. It won't eliminate every surprise, but it should make your first day a lot less stressful.

The following chapters offer a progressive, step-by-step process that will help you ease into a good church experience. While the steps are presented in a logical order, each stands on its own. You don't have to do every step I recommend in order for this book to be helpful. Just do the steps you want to do to make you feel more comfortable before visiting a Christian church. The point of this entire book is to help you feel prepared, to increase your chances of finding a church that's right for you, and to help you get the most out of your experience. You may be ready to visit a church with some confidence after just one step. If you want to do all the steps, that's okay, too. At any point, when you're ready to stop planning and start trying, go for it.

CHAPTER EIGHTEEN

Do a Little Under-the-Radar Research Before You Go

In chapter 1, I gave a list of beliefs a Christian church must adhere to and teach in order to be a Christian church. I urge you to keep that list handy as you begin researching possible churches to try out. I'll be pointing you back to that list in the chapters to come. You may have additional things you want to find out about any churches you might attend. But, again, I urge you not to attend a church that does not adhere to those must-have principles. They're that important.

Most people don't have the time to find out what every church within driving distance practices and teaches. So the first step in deciding which Christian church to visit is to narrow the field down to a manageable short list of possibilities so you can limit the research you'll need to do.

Maybe you've heard good things about a church in the media or from people you know who attend it. Put that church on the list. Maybe you've been at a church for a special event or a wedding and felt comfortable there. Note that church on your list.

Maybe you've seen a church's advertisements welcoming you to attend, and you had a good feeling about it. Put it on the list. Or, perhaps, there's simply a Christian church near your home that would be convenient to attend. Put that church on your list. Try to end up with a list of about five Christian churches you can look into further.

Once you have that, see what you can find out about each of the churches. Make a list of issues to research, starting with my list of must-haves in chapter 1 and adding any other questions that are important to you. Things like:

- Where is the church?
- What denomination is the church? (And what does that mean?)
- When are services?
- What is the style of worship?
- Does the church offer different services with different styles of worship?
- How big is the church? How many people attend services?
- Who is the pastor?
- Are there programs for your kids? When are they?
- Does the church address any special needs or physical limitations you may have?
- Does the church offer classes on topics that are important to you? (Divorce recovery, addiction recovery, parenting skills, financial planning, etc.)
- How do most people dress at services?
- Does the church offer rides for people without transportation?

These are just ideas of the kinds of things you might like to know before deciding which church to attend. Take away any that don't pertain to you, and add any you want so the list works for you. If you have five churches that are possibilities, I recommend making five copies of your list of questions, leaving room to fill in the answers as you find them out.

At the top of each, write down the church name, the phone number and the website address. Your local phone book or a two-minute search on the internet should get you that information for each church.

Once you have your blank information sheets, it's time to fill them in with the answers for each church. I highly recommend starting with the internet. Almost every church has a website. Open up your favorite search engine and type the name of the church and the city into the key words field. Find the link to the church's home page, and start exploring the website for your answers.

You'll likely find the answers to many—if not all—of your questions right on the website. If you're unable to find a website address for the church, call the church and ask for it.

On your information sheet, fill in all the answers to your questions that you can find on the website. Also, note any additional questions that come up as you read the content. Perhaps the website didn't give you a clear answer, or there's a class or special event the church mentions on its website you'd like to know more about.

If the website doesn't answer all your questions, click on the website's "contact us" link. Shoot the church an email saying you're researching some churches in the area and list your unanswered questions.

You might also ask them to mail you any background literature they offer and a statement of beliefs, if you haven't found that information on the website. A statement of beliefs should cover my list of must-haves from chapter 1. And it might include other information you'll find helpful.

The great thing about doing this under-the-radar research is that you can learn a lot without having to physically go to every church. Being a little organized and methodical about it helps keep the information straight, so you end up with a sheet for each church with answers to the same questions. This allows you to do an apples-to-apples comparison all from the comfort of your own home.

If you're still unclear about the differences among the various denominations of churches on your list, I suggest referring to other sources on the internet or in your local bookstore. Just search or ask for information on comparing Christian denominations. You might find a one-page comparison chart that tells you what you need to know.

There are also fine non-denominational churches, too. They adhere to all of the Christian church "must-haves" I listed in chapter 1, but they are not affiliated with a particular denomination.

Chances are good that this process will show you one or two of the five churches that best suit what you're looking for. You could just decide to try them out at this point. Or you can do more research on the top two churches.

CHAPTER NINETEEN

Speak to a Pastor Before You Go

I f you're still trying to narrow the list down to one or two churches to attend, or if you think you've got it figured out and just want to ask more questions before attending one, you might arrange a private meeting with a pastor.

Some churches will have you meet with the senior pastor. Some will have you meet with an associate pastor. Either is fine. A private meeting may sound intimidating for someone who's trying to tiptoe into church. But it needn't be. You might just find it less intimidating than showing up for your first church service surrounded by regular attendees—people you don't know.

If you do arrange a meeting, be honest about any skepticism you may still have about attending church or believing that the Bible really is the inspired Word of God. Most pastors will appreciate the honesty and that you're doing the research to make the right choice for you, even if that means you end up attending another church.

You can just lay your questions on the table and let the pastor answer them. Not only will you get more direct and well-explained answers than I give in this book—and that you found in your preliminary research—but you also can get a sense of the church's leadership style.

This meeting would be another great opportunity to ask about the church's denomination and how it differs from the denomination of another church you might be considering. It's a valid question to ask. If the church is non-denominational, you can ask the pastor why.

If it interests you, you could also ask for a tour of the church. What's the sanctuary like? Where are the classrooms where my kids will be during service? Where do they check in? These are all things that would be nice to find out while you're there before you actually attend a service for the first time.

CHAPTER TWENTY

Decide in Advance to
Visit Three Times

M any times, people attend a church for the first time at a special service. The church is putting on a well-publicized Easter service, Christmas program or a guest-speaker event that draws new people. The new people like what they find and start attending regular services. That's great. I'm all for it. But special services don't always give you a clear picture of what the church's regular Sunday (or Saturday) services are like. If you're really trying to evaluate a church, don't make a decision based on a special service.

You'll want to experience a church's regular service to see the style of worship, the flow of the service and how you respond to the regular pastor's teaching. You might not learn any of those things at a special service since they often feature performances or guest speakers. The only chance you might get to see or hear the regular pastor is when he offers the welcome and ending prayer—not enough to go on.

Whether your first attendance is at a special service or a regular service, I suggest that in advance you commit to attending at least three regular services before you decide if the church is one you'd like to continue attending. Why three? Well, remember, this is new to you. It might take one or two services for you to feel comfortable enough to absorb what's going on. Even if you're at the ideal church for you, it would be normal for you to be uncomfortable at first. It would be too bad if you mistook normal first-time discomfort for a bad fit.

Also, even regular services can vary from week to week. Maybe the pastor's topic doesn't interest you the first or second week. Then you find that in the third week the message connects with you on such a personal level that you're glad you showed up again. It happens all the time.

Another variable is the music. You may find the music too somber or too lively for your tastes one week, but completely gripping another week. I believe that it's a church's responsibility to teach its attendees about God and to lead them in the worship of God as God leads that church.

It's not the church's responsibility to alter its messages and music to our personal tastes. But there are teaching styles and music styles that connect with some and not with others. If these are things that will affect whether or not you continue attending a specific church, attending at least three times will help you avoid getting the wrong read from one service.

I'll again use the analogy of a new dating relationship. There are plenty of couples who have been happily married for many years whose first date was a total bomb. They couldn't stand each other. The only reason each person went on the second date was because they both lied at the end of the first one and said, "Well, that was nice. We'll have to go out again some time." And they were both too nice to lie again, so they went on the second date just to cut it off face-to-face.

Then, as they were both trying to convince each other that this thing had no future, they realized there was a hint of a future. Maybe that first date was doomed by a combination of jitters and an incorrect first impression. Forty-five years later, they're holding hands and laughing with their grandkids about the whole thing.

Getting to know a potential long-term church family is a lot like dating. Unless there are clear and obvious deal-breakers, don't rely on the first date to decide if you want to go steady. Remaining open to a better second, third and fourth impression is a more positive way to proceed. As your normal discomfort subsides, and as you attend your third service, you'll start to have a more accurate picture of what a church has to offer you—and perhaps what you have to offer the church.

Remember, commit to attending a church at least three times if you're really interested in finding one that's right for you.

CHAPTER TWENTY-ONE

Ask Someone You Know
to Go with You

L et's face it, we're chickens. Who is comfortable walking into a new situation alone, especially one in which you think everyone else already knows each other?

I don't know anyone—myself included—who wouldn't prefer a little moral support when crashing a party. I don't care if it's Alcoholics Anonymous, Weight Watchers or an Oscars viewing party. Sometimes we'd rather not take the step if we have to do it alone. But with a pal by your side, you're two. You can't be an odd man out if you're an even number.

If you'd like to attend a church, but you're just too uncomfortable showing up alone, don't. Ask a friend or family member to go with you. You can even tell him you're not expecting him to be a forever crutch. You just want a familiar face next to you one or two times. If he says no, remind him of the time you went with him somewhere you didn't want to go to give him moral support. It's what friends and family members do for each other.

Or perhaps you know someone, even a minor acquaintance, who already attends the church you want to try. Reintroduce yourself and let him know you're thinking of visiting his church. Chances are that he would be happy to meet you in the parking lot and show you around. You might even get a great tip as to where the coffee and donuts can be found after service. (Okay, now don't bail on a good church that doesn't offer coffee and donuts. It's not the key point here.)

The point is that there is absolutely no shame in needing a little support on your first day of any new endeavor. You know the old saying,

"Acclimation loves company." Yeah, I know that isn't it. But it's still true. Who knows? Maybe the friend you recruited will enjoy what he experiences and want to keep going with you.

You know the old saying, "Enjoyment loves company."

CHAPTER TWENTY-TWO

Pray Before You Go,
Even If You Don't Know How

Before you head out to church for the first time, have a chat with God. It's okay if you haven't prayed to Him before. If the idea makes you feel awkward or perhaps you're not even sure if you believe in God, do it anyway.

Remember, if you're seeking more meaning in your life, experiencing God is really the end goal of experiencing church. Church without God might be a nice social experience, but it won't transform your life. Only God can do that. So start your endeavor with some hope that He is real, and tell Him what's on your mind.

There's no approved script for prayer. You should only use "thee," "thou" and "doth" if you use those terms in your normal everyday speech. (Unless you're 400 years old, I'd guess you don't.) God likely isn't impressed with eloquence anyhow. He wants honesty. So be honest. Believe me, He won't be shocked by anything you say.

Find a place where you can be alone and just talk to Him. You can talk out loud or simply think the thoughts. He'll hear. Your prayer might sound something like this:

God, if You're real, then You know I'm not too sure about You. I have a lot of questions about You. For some reason, I'm feeling like it would be good for me to go to a Christian church. There are things in my life I need help with. I try to figure things out on my own, but I keep hitting walls. Sometimes I know what I should do, and don't do it. Sometimes I know what I shouldn't do, and I do it anyway. Sometimes, I just need help carrying the load. It's heavy, and I'm tired. If You are real, I hope You care about me, forgive me, and will help me get on the right path to better results in my life. I know I'm not going to get to know You any better without trying, so I am hoping that going to church will be a start. That's where they teach about You. Would You lead me to the right church and make it a good experience for me? Will You take a step toward me if I take this step toward You? You know I'm a little skeptical and nervous about going to church. Will You help me?

I just told you that there is no approved script, so this is just an example of a very honest prayer. Notice the lack of fancy words, Bible passages, or pretending a faith in Him that is not yet certain. It's just honest. God can work with that.

If you don't have a two-year-old son, imagine you do. Maybe he has a painful headache and comes to you for comfort. He doesn't know what causes the headache or how to fix it, so he goes to the only person he knows who can help him—you.

He raises his hands in the air for you to pick him up. Maybe he cries. All he can do is look at you, pat his own head and say, "Owie. Boo-boo."

It wouldn't even cross your mind to set him down and say, "I will not respond to such childish talk. You explain to me what you want in complete sentences and using specific medical terminology, or I will not even listen."

That would be absurd. Instead, you would have such compassion for your son that you'd do whatever you could to help ease his pain. You'd even feel the headache as if it were your own. He expressed a need as eloquently as he could. And he expressed it to you because he hopes you can help him.

We are God's two-year-old kids. He loves us even before we love Him. He desires to be our "Daddy" and delights when we go to Him for help, even when we don't know how to ask all that well. He's not expecting you to pray beyond your knowledge or level of faith in Him. He'll just be happy when you come to Him for help.

In the example I gave, there's another aspect of God that is modeled. Once you figure out that your son is telling you he has a headache, would you punish him for getting a headache? Would you shine a bright light in his eyes and clang cooking pots next to his ears? Of course not! You'd hold him, create a quiet, soothing environment, and maybe give him some children's pain medicine.

Likewise, God wants to ease our pain. He wants to help us learn and change the behavior that led to the pain in the first place. Even if the pain or struggles in our lives have been caused by our own poor decisions, He wants to forgive us and help us make better decisions in the future. He might require us to endure the consequences of our choices as a learning experience. But He'll hold our hands through the struggle, and He'll sit next to us on our beds and weep with us when it hurts. He'll feel our headache until it goes away.

Church is a great step toward a more positive, fulfilling and joyful life. That's the case because church is where you and others like you can learn about a very real God who wants that better life for you. You may not be as sure of this as I am just yet. Your willingness to explore the possibility is enough right now. Saying a simple, honest prayer—something like the example I provided—will help set your mind on the right track beforehand. And it will reach the ears of a loving Daddy who will respond.

If you do say a prayer, don't be concerned if you don't have an awe-inspiring, supernatural experience or if all your problems aren't solved at your first visit to church. It doesn't mean your prayer wasn't heard, that God isn't real, or that He isn't already at work in your life.

Sometimes God answers prayer immediately and in a big way. More often, though, His answers come over time and through a process He wants us to experience. He knows the best way to cure the headaches in our lives and to teach us how to avoid them in the future. He may choose to do it in a way you don't expect or even like. What child likes taking medicine? Just remember that two-year-olds don't always see the big picture like Daddy does.

So pray however you can best communicate how you feel and what you want. Then take a step toward Him by going to church. Have hope that He's already taken a step toward you. Get ready to smile when you find out that He takes bigger steps than you.

CHAPTER TWENTY-THREE

Be Friendly, but Sit in the Back (It's Okay)

If you've been reading through these chapters in order, I've twice used the example of a self-righteous church lady sitting behind you during services. To exaggerate my points, I told you that if she hits you with her purse because you're not being "churchy" enough, you should whack her back. My sincere belief is that you'll never really get into a slugfest with a cranky old lady in church. I'm simply using absurdity to address some unfounded fears many people have about what church might be like.

However, in my attempt to assuage your possible fears, I might have raised one you never had. If you didn't before, perhaps now you have this vision of people sitting behind you in church watching your every move. You imagine feeling the burn of their eyes on the back of your scalp as they quietly criticize you for not looking holy enough. Maybe they'll even confront you— Oh, wait. I'm doing it again. Perhaps I should just say that no matter where you sit, you'll probably find only nice people all around you who are just happy you're there. But one surefire way to eliminate the fear of being watched is to sit in the back row.

Really. It's okay. Just get there early and have your choice of prime back-row seating. There's nothing terribly antisocial or unholy about sitting in the back row. If the church fills up, someone will have to sit there. Why not you? Look at it as a service to someone else who'd rather have a spot closer to the action.

Sitting in the back is a great way to ensure that no one will be evaluating your church attendance skills from behind. It also puts you in position to absorb the whole church in front of you. You're there to learn. No harm in putting more of the lesson in front of you so you can learn more.

However, as you attend church, I hope you don't send signals that you want to be left alone. While I suggest sitting in the back if you're more comfortable, I'd still recommend exchanging friendly greetings with other parishioners. If the pastor says it's time to shake hands and say good morning, make it a point to join in even if you have to walk forward a row or two. If you left a church after a visit and no one seemed friendly toward you or said hello, you might feel let down. So, by all means, don't present an air of being unapproachable.

Most churchgoers are nice people who wouldn't feel right bothering someone who looked as though they wanted to be left alone. Sitting in the back and having a warm smile on your face is a great way to ease into church while remaining approachable.

Now, because churchgoers tend to be such nice people, you might get some well-intentioned usher or attendee who feels bad for you sitting way in the back. Be prepared for someone who might urge you to move up. "Hey, there. No need to sit way back there. Why don't you come on toward the front? There's plenty of room."

If that sounds nice to you, great. Move on up. But if the idea of moving up makes you uncomfortable, just say with a big smile, "Oh. Thanks so much. But I really prefer being able to take everything in from back here." That ought to end it with no one feeling awkward.

In the interest of full disclosure, you might encounter someone who's a little more persistent. Let me urge you to hold off on whacking that person until it's a last resort. Instead, let me offer some other things to say that will make your intention to stay in the back row clear without resorting to violence:

- "I've got the bladder of a hamster and need to be able to duck out on short notice. But thanks."
- "I brought the wrong glasses. Wouldn't be able to see a thing if I sit near the front. But thanks."

- "This exact spot has special meaning to me. But thanks." (Let them wonder all service what that's about.)
- "I read a book by a guy who said the back row is a great place to sit if you're visiting a church and don't want to get whacked by a self-righteous church lady sitting behind you. I'm going to stay here and try it out. But thanks."

I'm not encouraging you to lie. Pick one that's true. Or come up with one of your own. At the very least, these are fun to think up. But don't worry. If you look happily situated in the back row, you probably won't encounter even one person who urges you to move forward. And if you do, you're first "no thanks" will likely end it peacefully.

CHAPTER TWENTY-FOUR

Have an Open Mind and a Focused Mind

Have you ever had a disagreement with someone and been so committed to your point of view that you never really even listened to his argument? You might have stopped talking while his lips moved, but you were too busy thinking about your next point that you never heard his. Have you ever done that and found out later that you were wrong? Worse yet, you would have realized you were wrong during the initial discussion if you had only listened with the intent of honestly understanding what your opponent was saying. Ouch.

I wish I could say that never happened to me. It has—and it does. We humans have a strong desire to be right. This desire can be so powerful that sometimes we slam our brains shut when someone wants to offer another opinion. Sure, we go through the appearance of listening to seem respectful. But it's very easy to forget how important it is to actually listen. Sometimes the other person is right. Sometimes it's about something too big to get wrong, but we won't listen because our brains are padlocked.

Throughout this book, I've told you it's okay to go to church if you don't believe everything I've told you about Christianity. When I first went, not only did I not believe some of what was being taught, I had not even heard much of it. Over time, I became a believer. I think that timeframe could have been greatly reduced—and the blessing could have come a lot sooner—if I had chosen to start going to church with a more open attitude.

I spent much of my early time at church not really listening to learn. Far too often, I was waiting for the pastor to teach something I disagreed with so I could debate him in my mind. Of course, eventually I found out he was right and then regretted the time I wasted being wrong and carrying a chip on my shoulder. I've included this chapter because I'd like to spare you this regret.

If you're unsure about Christianity, don't waste your time at church with a closed mind. Go with the expectation that you're there to honestly learn what is being taught. Even more, go with the hope that what is being taught is right and, if it is, it's too important to miss. Decide before you get to church that you're a student intent on understanding the material and completely open to its truth. Be aware of the human tendency to protect our old way of thinking and to dismiss any challenges to it. If you don't open your mind consciously, it will be too easy for you to close your mind subconsciously.

If you go with this attitude, you'll learn better. It doesn't mean you'll be tricked into believing anything. When I'm at my best, I can listen intently to someone with a completely different opinion than my own. I decide that I genuinely want to understand his point of view with an open mind. I consciously disable my prideful, protective, defensive, argumentative shields so I can hear what he's saying.

Sometimes when I do this, I realize his opinion is right. I may have "lost" an argument, but I'm better for it because I heard, understood and ultimately agreed with a different point of view than I had held. Sometimes, however, after giving the other person his best shot at a willing listener, I still disagree. And I'm still better for it, because my resolve on the matter is even stronger. I walk away with more information than I had before and my own position further supported. If we're more interested in discovering truth than being right, listening with an open mind is the way to go.

Once you decide to have an open mind, you also have to try to have a focused mind. You can have the best intentions in the world, but if your attention drifts, the new information will never reach your cerebral gray matter.

At church, there is no shortage of distractions to lure your mind away from the pastor's teaching. The pews are filled with other people, and people-watching is a universal favorite pastime. People are funny, odd, oddly matched, interesting, out-of-place, eerily familiar, noisy, antsy, overly expressive, inappropriately dressed, and writing notes that you'd like to eyeball. You've got to be pretty focused to pass up a show like that. Try!

Then, if you can avoid visual distractions, you've also got to avoid the mental ones. I admit that I have to work at this. My poor pastor can be teaching an important message—one he spent a week of study and prayer to prepare—and my mind can be grappling with what I plan to have for lunch after the service. It's very easy to leave church having missed the most important part of the service: the teaching of the Bible.

I've told you that the social aspect of church is nice, but it's not the life-changing stuff. What the pastor is teaching is the life-changing stuff. Don't take the teaching lightly.

Your reasons for wanting to explore Christian church are your own. Whatever they are, they probably include wanting to improve the quality of your life in some way your old habits have not provided. That means you're seeking a new point of view. If you go into it with your shields up, you might end up repelling the one point of view that not only offers what you seek, but also offers possibly more than you ever even imagined.

Having an open mind will give you your best opportunity to understand the message. Staying focused on the message while you're in church will ensure that it reaches your open mind. Then you will be in a better position to accept or reject it when the time comes.

CHAPTER TWENTY-FIVE

Ask Questions About Things You Don't Understand

E ven after attending church and studying the Bible for many years, I still find that sometimes my pastor or my Bible raises issues I don't understand at first blush.

If you're new to a Christian church, expect that this will happen to you from time to time. You're simply not going to hear or read everything once and process it perfectly. Some of the concepts are so radical—so different from how the world portrays the Christian faith—that they have to swim upstream against powerful currents to reach a place of understanding in our brains. When these questions come up, try to get answers. Leaving the sanctuary confused and arriving for the next service still confused isn't the best way to learn.

It's always good to have a pen and notepad handy during the service. That way, you can jot down scripture references and sermon points that you'll want to remember. You should also write down the points you find unclear. During the week, try to reread the scripture that the material was based on.

Many Bibles have notes at the bottom of the pages or even in columns in the text that provide a commentary on the scripture text. Those notes are there to help you understand a difficult passage. Some Bibles have a concordance in the back that lists key words you'll find in the Bible and includes all or most scripture references where the word is used. Studying the Bible verses listed there will give you a good idea of the concept a particular word conveys, hopefully shedding light on a concept that has you puzzled.

You can also do a little search engine work online and find commentary there. Just be sure you're at a reputable Christian website before taking the commentary to heart.

Perhaps you can find the pastor's email address on the church's website or in the church bulletin and email your questions directly. The pastor will likely appreciate that you cared enough about his sermon to follow up. Chances are good you'll get a response that you'll find helpful.

It's also quite possible you're not the only one who didn't quite absorb the original explanation during the service. Maybe the pastor will choose to expand on his explanation during the next sermon and you will have helped other people who have the same question. Remember my example of church being like the schoolhouse on *Little House on the Prairie*. Everyone is there to learn. Don't be afraid to ask the question others might be thinking.

Perhaps you know someone you consider to be a mature, knowledgeable Christian. Don't be shy about asking him for his take on your questions. You might feel more comfortable chatting with someone you know rather than contacting the pastor or trying to find answers on your own.

I'm never embarrassed to ask another believer for input on something I'm not quite sure about. Nor am I ever put off by someone asking me for my input. I enjoy talking about the things I've learned and experienced. Sometimes I find that I don't have a good answer to the questions, and it wakes me up to my own need to continue learning. Finding the answer helps the person who asks the question and the person who is asked.

Whatever you do, don't think of this as having to do extra homework. This isn't algebra and you won't have to stay back a year if you don't pass the test. Rather, you're exploring the revelation of God to humanity. Your understanding of what you learn is key to attaining the benefits you hope knowing more about God might bring to your life. You are seeking a treasure.

Have fun as you learn to understand the treasure map—the Bible. You may not accept every piece of information as truth right away—or ever, for that matter. Your acceptance of it is completely between you and God. But do your best to understand scripture passages or concepts with which you struggle. Be sure that your eventual decision to accept or reject the concepts is based on knowledge, not confusion.

CHAPTER TWENTY-SIX

Read the Bulletin
and Fill out the Contact Card

If the usher or greeter at the church you attend hands you a church bulletin, take a moment to read it.

You might want to hold onto that baby with your stronger hand clenched tightly over one of the open sides. At my church, there is a separate loose insert for every class and outreach activity the church has going on at that time. The inserts are either slippery or spring-loaded. They tend to fly out like a deck of cards in a good game of "52 Pick-Up." It's hard to look cool and blend in when you're chasing a bulletin full of inserts around the sanctuary floor.

The bulletin and each insert can be very helpful in your quest to learn what this particular church is all about. Churches have new resources and participation opportunities all the time.

Even if you're not interested in those opportunities, you can get a good sense of what this church provides its attendees, its community and the world through missions work. You might also learn names of church staff and volunteers and their respective roles. Better yet, you might find a class or an event that is right up your alley. Don't expect that you'll hear about every opportunity during the announcements before or after the pastor's sermon. Churches try to keep those announcements brief. That's why they provide the bulletins.

A lot of churches ask newcomers and even regular attendees to fill out a contact card, which is often in the bulletin or in the pew rack. The card might ask you if you have any prayer requests or if you want information on certain classes or topics, like baptism or Bible studies offered during the week.

Instead of a contact card, some churches have a folder at the end of each row and they ask everyone to sign it. Either way, you won't be asked to do anything different from every other person in attendance.

Many churches want to make sure visitors feel welcomed at the church, so they contact visitors later in the week by either phone or letter just to thank them for visiting and ask if they have any questions. Unless you're trying to fly way under the radar for some reason, I suggest that you fill out the contact card or sign-in folder and see how the church follows up.

It might even make you feel better about the church you attended if you get a nice call from a friendly person or a letter saying, "Thanks for coming. Hope to see you again!" If you don't mind filling out the contact card or sign-in folder but really do not want to be contacted, just make it clear with a note that says, "Do not wish to be contacted. Thank you."

I cannot speak for every church, but most will be respectful of anything you write. And I'd be surprised if even one church in the country would ever share your information with another organization. So that's really nothing to worry about. The contact card simply helps the church hear of needs or requests of parishioners. A church can only respond to these needs if the church knows about them. Likewise, a church can only welcome new visitors if it knows they visited.

Churches also use the contact card to track attendance trends and needs of its attendees to make important decisions about its facilities and staffing. So when you fill out the contact card, you're helping the church help you and others.

CHAPTER TWENTY-SEVEN

Hang Around After the Service to See How Folks Interact

One thing I love about being at church is seeing how much the people enjoy each other. I'm blessed to be at a church where a good percentage of people attending the service hang around in the sanctuary, the lobby and the patio area to talk. It's a crowded scene of group chats, laughter and even serious, heartfelt conversations.

This fits my personality perfectly since I like making the rounds to catch up on the news with many people I truly enjoy, but whom I only see once or twice a week. For me, my church is the equivalent of some people's Friday night cocktail parties. It's not a place I have to be as an obligation to endure. It's a place where I genuinely enjoy hanging out. I suppose not every church has such a light and lively atmosphere. But I'm glad mine does.

You might find that the "after-service" atmosphere offers you more insight about whether you're at a church that's right for you. When you visit, instead of bolting out to the parking lot and leaving a patch of rubber to the exit, why not hang around for a while and check out the vibes?

I absolutely would do this if I were checking out a new church. Even if I didn't know another soul well enough to engage in a conversation of my own, I'd want to see if and how many attendees did. If very few attendees stick around to visit with each other on a friendship level, that tells you something. Perhaps the church has a more serious, less collegial style. Maybe it has fewer opportunities for parishioners to get to know each other on a more personal level. These are not necessarily bad things. Perhaps that's more your style. But you can't really learn that if you leave right after the service.

If your style is more like mine, you'll want to see if people seem to know each other and like each other. I think church should be a place of friendship and laughter. I know that this atmosphere comes from the top, down. If the leadership of the church has a joyful vision, the parishioners will too.

To me, a warm, familiar atmosphere also means that the church is active, with many opportunities for its people to participate at a more intimate level than simply attending services. This is the kind of church that inspires me to get plugged in and help move the church forward. It's fun and rewarding. It gives me a sense of belonging.

This brings me to an important point: When you first start visiting a church, you may not know people, and they might not know you. So be fair. Don't expect people to include you in personal conversations just because you're in the vicinity. It does not mean they are rude or exclusionary. It just means they are human and don't know you.

I would love for every visitor to a church to be greeted warmly and genuinely as a new friend. And that might happen on a first visit if you present yourself as friendly and open to interaction.

But don't get offended if it doesn't happen for a while. If you observe a fun and lively atmosphere—like the one I described at my church—but feel like you're on the outside looking in, chalk it up to human nature, not cliquishness. Realize that most of the people you see laughing it up together have had the opportunity to get to know each other by participating in smaller group activities at the church.

Until you get involved in some of those activities, other attendees might not have the privilege of getting to know you. So while they might offer a warm hello to a new face, they might not drag you into their group under the assumption that you want to be introduced around.

I know I'm not terribly comfortable striking up a conversation with someone I don' know. Maybe that person wouldn't be comfortable with it either. So observing to see how others interact is a good way to see what kind of social opportunities wait for you if and when you're willing to get involved with others in various church activities. But please don't get your feelings hurt because you're not immediately invited into the intimate camaraderie.

When you add your after-service observations to your impressions of the service, you'll get a broader picture of the church's atmosphere. Then you can make a more informed decision about whether a church is right for your personal style.

CHAPTER TWENTY-EIGHT

See If There Are Special Classes or Resources on Subjects that Interest You

So how do you get more plugged in, get to know other people better and get the most out of what your church has to offer? I'm glad you asked. The answer is, "Ask."

If you have a certain gift or passion—like caring for children—ask if the church needs help with child care during its services or other events. (Note: Don't be put off if they talk to you about background checks and training before you work with children. It has nothing to do with you; it's about complying with safety, insurance and liability issues. In fact, I would hesitate to be part of a church that doesn't have those safeguards in place for those working with a vulnerable population.)

Working in that area will be something you enjoy and help the church immensely. You'll get to know the kids, church staffers, other volunteers and the parents of the children.

Or maybe it's singing in the choir, pitching in to provide or serve food at a church event or helping direct traffic in the parking lot. Maybe you're good with your hands and can help with a building project or creating some scenery for the Easter musical. Simply think of what you enjoy doing and ask if the church has a need that matches.

If you're on a quest to improve your knowledge of the Bible and the Christian faith, ask if the church has additional teaching sessions available. The larger the church, the more likely it is to have an array of study opportunities. But even smaller churches tend to have midweek Bible studies. Sometimes they are at the church and taught by the pastor. Sometimes they are small groups that meet at the church, in homes or at a local coffee shop.

I have been involved in group Bible studies for many years and likely will continue to be involved in them for the rest of my life. In addition to attaining a much deeper understanding of the Bible, this is where I have formed my closest relationships over the years. My fellow students have become my closest friends because we have been able to get to know each other and care for each other on a deeper level.

Some opportunities to develop friendships are based purely on hobbies. Do you like to play golf? Participate in the church's golf tournament if it has one. Or maybe your church needs a shortstop for its softball team. Perhaps a group of people at the church has a common interest that has nothing to do with the church. One guy at my church is a gun enthusiast and put out a little flyer that invited other enthusiasts to join him at a local target range. In no time at all, he had a large group of new friends sharing his hobby with him. Through that, they're all getting to know each other as individuals rather than nameless "other attendees" at Sunday services.

Do you like quilting bees, poetry, jogging, walking, ballroom dancing, painting, book clubs, recipe swaps, cigars, going to professional baseball games, hot rods, kiddie play groups, board games, hacky sack, flying disc golf or making music? Maybe others at the church do, too.

The point is that you might be surprised at the interests you have in common with other people at the church. If you want to meet people who share your interests, ask someone if there is already a group centered around that hobby or activity. Maybe the church will help you put the word out if you'd like to get one started. What church wouldn't love to boast a large, active group of hacky sackers?

When you find a way to get connected to other people at the church, you give other people an opportunity to get connected to you. And this is where you can have some real fun and develop quality friendships with wonderful people. Then you'll be one of those people engaged in fun conversations after the service. You'll also have other people who are learning to get closer to God that you can call when you need a companion, a prayer or a word of encouragement.

CHAPTER TWENTY-NINE

Try Another Church If the First Doesn't Suit You

My hope is that you feel right at home in the first church you visit—that you'll go at least three times and want to keep on going. You'll be there a while and find ways to get involved beyond just attending service. You'll make friends. You'll be home.

But if that doesn't happen—perhaps you give it your best effort and find that it's just not where you want to be—don't give up your search. Brush off your notes from your original under-the-radar research (see chapter 18) and try another church.

Resist any temptation you may have to give up on church, the Bible, faith and a relationship with Jesus. Remember that your old life and your old attitudes about these things weren't working for you in the first place. Don't go quietly back to your old rut. Trust that continuing your exploration of Christianity will lead you to your real purpose in this life and the next. Perhaps you visited a very good church, but it just wasn't the right one for you. It happens. Stir up a renewed hope and a great attitude, and take them with you to another church.

I mentioned before that there are many solid Christian churches in many different denominations and that there are even different service styles within a single denomination. Big churches. Small churches. Loud churches. Quiet churches. Formal churches. Casual churches. Lots of good churches. Lots of different experiences. If you're searching with the right attitude and you have asked God to help you find a church family, I believe you'll find one you can call home.

I will say that you should not expect to find a church that has no faults.

That is an unrealistic goal. All churches will have some aspects you'll like and some you won't. If you live on earth, you know that the best marriages involve two people who really care about each other and who choose to accept each other's shortcomings. We call them "perfect marriages," not because the two people are perfect but because they're committed to taking the bad with the good and to lifting each other up instead of tearing each other down.

If two people go into marriage ready to bail if the other leaves the toilet seat up or burns the roast, they never had realistic expectations of marriage. In the same way, being a part of a church is like a marriage. If you want your church to accept you with your little faults, accept your church with its little faults. Do this, and you'll have the opportunity to experience a lifelong relationship that makes both of you better. When I suggest trying another church if the first doesn't suit you, I'm talking about a seriously bad fit, not little imperfections.

CHAPTER THIRTY

Make It About Him, Not You

Throughout this book, I have acknowledged that you have some desire for change in your life that has prompted you to consider going to a Christian church. If that wasn't the case, I don't think you would have opened this book in the first place. And, for sure, you wouldn't still be reading.

Even if you're not sure you understand or will ultimately believe what is taught, you're open to the idea that what you have been looking for might be found in church and through the teaching of the Bible. By reading this book, you've proven that you're genuinely interested in exploring a Christian church with the intent of making it the first step toward a new life. You're willing to overcome apathy, uncertainty or even negative attitudes about the Christian church in order to, hopefully, receive the blessings it could bring to your life. Let me say to you, as one who once was standing in the exact same place many years ago, it's time to go and see for yourself.

I have given you all of the "inside information" I wish someone had given me when I was in your shoes. I have given it to you as openly and directly as I know how. I hope I have opened your eyes to a new perspective on some of the most common hang-ups and excuses people use to avoid church and in the process convinced you that these are based more on rationalizing their decisions than on reality.

I told you that the living God loves you, wants you to accept Him as your own, wants to forgive you and welcome you into His arms for the rest of your life and for an eternity after that. He has given you the Bible (His

Word) and the church (His family) to bless you. I've even given you a step-by-step process to help you narrow your search for a church and find the one that you might one day call home. I've done my best to share all the little things you might want to know before you get there, the things that will make you feel more prepared and at ease during your first visit, as well as the things that will make your experience more fulfilling for years to come. I know the blessings will be there for you if you take the step.

Now, let me reiterate the most important word of advice I have given you in these pages. You may be going to church to receive blessings. That's good. But the real blessings come from giving. At some point, I hope you give more than your Sunday mornings to a church. I hope you give the reins of your life to Jesus Christ.

If you don't know Him already, look for Him at church. Seek Him in His Word. Listen for His leading as you quiet yourself to think about Him. Cry with Him when you sense His pain for a world that rejects His love. Laugh with Him when you feel His joy during songs of worship. Respond when He calls you to come to Him.

You might experience some benefits by simply attending church. But you will receive a new life from the only one who can give it. Jesus Christ is who He says He is. I know it, now. Make your search—your church experience—about finding Him more than about finding life-changing "tips," and you'll find a life-changing Friend.

Start the search for the treasure you've been seeking. It's time to go to church.

A Final Word from the Author

I n this book, I've explained what it means to be "saved" by accepting Jesus Christ as your Lord and Savior. And I've suggested that it's okay to go to church if you're not ready to make this step because church is a great place to learn more about it.

However, I did not explain how to accept Christ when you're ready to take this wonderful step of faith. So I decided to add this instruction if you're ready now, or if you become ready in the future. I sincerely hope you do. And I sincerely hope this helps.

The italicized text that follows the next paragraph offers words for a simple prayer. If you say these words to God and truly mean them, truly believe that you are forgiven, and truly give Him your life, you will be saved.

You will be His, and He will send His Holy Spirit to live in your heart to comfort you, help you, teach you, correct you and lead you in His service. You can use your own words, of course. But don't bargain will Jesus. You must accept Him on His terms, or you're not really accepting Him. Don't worry, though. His terms are perfect.

Jesus, please forgive me of all my sins. Forgive the sins I've done, spoken and thought throughout all my life. Forgive the sins I will commit in the future as I struggle against myself, the temptations of this world and Satan himself. I believe that You carried these sins, my sins, on the cross. I believe that You bled and died to pay for my sins so that I could be saved. I believe You were raised from the dead and You are alive today. Thank You for washing me clean. I believe I am clean in Your eyes right now and forevermore, even when I stumble. Now help me turn from sin and become more like You every day. Help me learn Your truth and apply it to my life. Help me live in the joy of knowing You love me and that I am Yours. Thank You for preparing for me a place in heaven that I could never earn, but that I receive today. Help me to follow You and to serve You all the days of my life. Help me to never be ashamed of You or the good news of Your Holy Word. Thank You, my Lord and Savior, Jesus. I love You. Thank You for loving me.

If and when you say this prayer, or one like it, and mean it with all your heart…welcome home. I'll see you in heaven.